INTRODUCTION

JOURNEY INTO SOUTH AMERICA'S NA

Have you ever dreamed of stepping into a world where _...._ as far as the eye can see, snow-capped peaks tower over ancient valleys, and vibrant cultures pulse with a history as rich as the land itself? South America's natural wonders are not just breathtaking landscapes—they're living stories waiting to be explored.

From the sprawling Amazon rainforest, home to countless species found nowhere else on earth, to the rugged Andes mountains that cradle hidden ecosystems, this continent is a treasure trove of ecological riches. But it's more than just nature's beauty—these lands carry the spirit and traditions of indigenous peoples who have safeguarded them for centuries. In 2025, South American park tourism is evolving, blending adventure with respect, and inviting travelers to experience these wonders in new, sustainable ways.

This guide and atlas are designed to be your trusted companion on this journey. Inside, you'll find detailed maps and trail descriptions, carefully curated highlights of each park, and essential trip-planning advice. Whether you're navigating dense jungle paths or high-altitude treks, safety tips and environmental guidelines will help you travel responsibly—so that these incredible places remain vibrant for generations to come.

Preparing for your South American adventure means more than packing the right gear—it means understanding the climates you'll encounter, from tropical heat to mountain chill, knowing the vaccinations and permits required, and embracing the customs and etiquette that make each community unique. With thoughtful preparation and an open heart, your journey will be not only unforgettable but respectful and enriching.

So, get ready to embark on an adventure that will transform how you see the world—and yourself. South America's natural wonders await.

CHAPTER 1

AMAZON RAINFOREST NATIONAL PARKS – LUNGS OF THE EARTH

Have you ever wondered what it truly means to breathe in the lungs of our planet? To walk where the air is thick with life, where every breath you take connects you to an ancient rhythm pulsing through billions of leaves, rivers, and creatures? This is the Amazon rainforest — a colossal, living heart of the Earth, and a place so immense, so vibrant, it defies comprehension.

I remember the first time I stepped beneath the emerald canopy of Manu National Park in Peru. The air was heavy with humidity and a thousand whispered calls from unseen animals. My excitement was electric. I had read about these forests, seen pictures, heard stories from locals and seasoned explorers. But nothing, absolutely nothing, prepared me for the raw, overwhelming reality of being there. It was like stepping into a world that existed beyond time, where every leaf, every insect, every glint of light was part of an intricate dance as old as the planet itself.

If you've ever dreamt of exploring the Amazon's iconic national parks — Manu in Peru, Yasuni in Ecuador, and Madidi in Bolivia — this chapter is your gateway. These parks are not just protected areas on a map.

South America
National Parks 2025

Ultimate Travel Guide & Atlas to Rainforests, Mountains, Wildlife, Hiking Trails, and Scenic Outdoor Adventures

Disclaimer and Terms of Use

The author and publisher of this book and the accompanying materials have used their best efforts in preparing this book. The author and publisher make no representation or warranties with respect to the accuracy, applicability, fitness, or completeness of the contents of this book. The information contained in this book is strictly for informational purposes. Therefore, if you wish to apply the ideas contained in this book, you are taking full responsibility for your actions.

Printed in the United States of America

TABLE OF CONTENT

They are sanctuaries of biodiversity, home to species found nowhere else, cradling ancient cultures, and presenting challenges and rewards unlike anywhere else on earth.

EXPLORING THE VAST TROPICAL RAINFOREST: WHY THESE PARKS ARE UNMATCHED

You've probably heard the Amazon described as the "lungs of the Earth." But what does that really mean? It means this forest alone produces about 20% of the world's oxygen. It is the largest continuous tropical rainforest on the planet, spanning over 5.5 million square kilometers. It's so vast, it stretches across nine countries and countless indigenous territories.

What's more, the Amazon is a global biodiversity hotspot, with estimates suggesting that up to 10% of the world's known species call it home. And within this sprawling wilderness, Manu, Yasuni, and Madidi stand out as crown jewels, each offering a unique window into the richness and mystery of the rainforest.

Manu National Park — Peru's Ecological Treasure

Manu is more than just a park — it's a UNESCO World Heritage site that encompasses everything from the lowland Amazon jungle to the high Andes foothills. Visiting Manu feels like traveling through multiple worlds in one journey.

What I found unforgettable during my visit was the staggering variety of life packed into this one area. On a canopy walk that lifted me over the treetops, I spotted brilliantly colored macaws squawking in the morning light, capuchin monkeys swinging from branch to branch, and the rare sight of a harpy eagle — one of the largest and most powerful raptors in the world.

Manu's river systems are arteries of life, teeming with pink river dolphins, giant otters, and countless fish species. And at night, the forest transforms into a symphony of insects, frogs, and other nocturnal creatures, so alive that the darkness itself seems electric.

One insider's tip: Manu's dry season, from May to October, offers the best conditions for wildlife spotting and trekking. The trails are more accessible, and the rivers are lower, making river excursions easier and safer. I was there in June, and every moment felt like a discovery.

Yasuni National Park — Ecuador's Hidden Jewel

Yasuni is often described as one of the most biodiverse places on the planet — and with good reason. I had the privilege of joining an indigenous Kichwa guide who shared his intimate knowledge of the forest. He explained how every plant, every animal, has a role in the complex ecosystem, and how his people have lived in harmony with the forest for generations.

What makes Yasuni truly remarkable is the sheer number of species packed into this relatively small area. From frogs with colors so vivid they look painted, to elusive jaguars and rare orchids that bloom only under certain moon phases, the park is a living classroom of nature's wonders.

If you want to experience Yasuni, the best months are between August and November when the weather is drier and trails are easier to navigate. But be prepared: much of Yasuni is remote and undeveloped, so guided tours are essential for safety and a richer experience.

Madidi National Park — Bolivia's Biodiversity Powerhouse

Madidi feels like the wild heart of the Amazon. I was fortunate enough to take a multi-day expedition into the park, and it was one of the most challenging — and exhilarating — journeys I have ever undertaken.

Madidi covers everything from dense rainforests to high-altitude cloud forests and rivers that pulse with energy. It's estimated to be home to over 1,000 bird species alone, including the majestic Andean cock-of-the-rock, which I watched perform its courtship dance one early morning in a misty clearing.

One of the most astonishing parts of Madidi is how varied the ecosystems are. As we ascended into higher elevations, the landscape changed dramatically, and with it the plants and animals. This transition is a photographer's dream and a naturalist's paradise.

From my experience, the best time to visit Madidi is during the dry season from May to September. This season makes it easier to explore both the jungle and mountainous areas without battling relentless rain and muddy trails.

Rivers, Canopy Walks, and Biodiversity Hotspots

If you want to truly grasp the Amazon, you have to understand its rivers. These vast waterways are the lifeblood of the forest, carving paths through dense jungle, shaping ecosystems, and sustaining countless species. When I first took a canoe ride down the Madre de Dios river in Manu, I felt like I was floating through a living artery, with water so dark and deep it mirrored the towering trees above.

In all three parks, river tours are the best way to access hidden areas teeming with wildlife. Look out for giant river otters playing in the water, schools of colorful fish darting beneath the surface, and the occasional splash of a caiman disappearing into the reeds.

Canopy walks are another incredible way to experience the forest. Suspended high above the forest floor, these walkways reveal a world few people ever see. The canopy is where much of the rainforest's biodiversity thrives — fruits, flowers, and insects in a vibrant, sun-drenched world. From my personal experience, standing on a canopy tower at dawn and watching the sun illuminate the misty leaves is nothing short of magical.

Biodiversity hotspots within these parks are places where species diversity reaches extraordinary levels. Guides will often take you to areas known for specific plants or animals. In Yasuni, for instance, certain trails lead to rare orchid blooms or frog populations that scientists still study. Madidi's diverse elevation gradients allow visitors to see species adapted to vastly different habitats in a single day's hike.

Best Times to Visit and Guided Tours: Making the Most of Your Experience

Timing your trip is crucial to having an unforgettable and safe Amazon experience. The Amazon has two main seasons — wet and dry — and each offers a very different perspective.

The wet season, roughly from November to April, transforms the forest into a flooded wonderland. Trails become rivers, animals disperse widely, and the landscape pulses with life in ways impossible during drier months. Yet, traveling can be harder, and mosquitoes are far more relentless. From my own trip during the early wet season, I learned the importance of patience and preparation.

The dry season, from May to October, offers easier access, better hiking conditions, and generally more predictable weather. Wildlife viewing can be excellent as animals gather around shrinking water sources. Personally, I recommend this season for first-timers or those seeking more comfort in their adventure.

Guided tours are non-negotiable when exploring these parks. Local guides possess priceless knowledge — from spotting elusive creatures to understanding the plants used for medicine or food. I remember one day in Manu when our guide pointed out a tiny leaf insect so perfectly camouflaged I would have walked past it a hundred times without noticing.

For an immersive experience, consider multi-day expeditions that combine hiking, canoeing, and cultural visits to indigenous communities. These tours reveal the true soul of the Amazon, going beyond the surface to connect you deeply with this extraordinary ecosystem.

Insider Advice: What I Wish I Knew Before Going

I won't sugarcoat it — exploring the Amazon is challenging. The humidity can be suffocating, the insects relentless, and the terrain unforgiving. But the rewards are life-changing.

Before my first trip, I underestimated how physically demanding the jungle would be. I was exhausted but exhilarated after long hikes, soaking wet from sudden tropical downpours. What kept me going was a blend of curiosity and respect for the forest.

Here are some insider tips from my experience:

- Pack lightweight, quick-dry clothing and bring layers for cooler mornings or evenings. A good hat and high-quality mosquito repellent are essential.

- Hydration is key. Always carry enough water and use purification tablets or filters for natural sources.
- Carry a good pair of waterproof hiking boots, and break them in before the trip to avoid blisters.
- Invest in a reliable waterproof bag for your electronics and important documents.
- Learn basic phrases in Spanish and, if possible, some local indigenous words — it goes a long way with guides and communities.
- Be mentally prepared to unplug. There is little to no phone service deep in the parks, which is a blessing in disguise.

WILDLIFE WATCHING AND BOTANICAL WONDERS

Have you ever stood in the dense green silence of the Amazon rainforest, heart pounding as the unmistakable rustle of leaves signals that something wild and magnificent is near? Imagine spotting a jaguar — that elusive, regal predator — emerge from the shadows, or hearing the piercing, vibrant calls of macaws soaring overhead in a symphony of color. This is not a distant dream. This is the reality of wildlife watching in the Amazon's most treasured national parks.

During my many treks through Manu, Yasuni, and Madidi, I was repeatedly overwhelmed by the richness of life around me. It felt as if the forest itself was alive in a way I had never experienced before, every inch teeming with movement, sound, and color. I wasn't just a visitor; I was a witness to one of the most spectacular natural theaters on Earth. But there's a deeper story here — a story of conservation, indigenous wisdom, and a delicate balance that allows these wonders to flourish.

Jaguars: The Ghosts of the Forest

If there is one animal that defines the mystique of the Amazon, it is undoubtedly the jaguar. These magnificent cats are apex predators, masters of stealth and power, yet rarely seen by humans. When I first caught sight of a jaguar on a guided night safari in Madidi, my excitement was beyond words.

You have to understand how rare and precious this moment is. Jaguars are solitary creatures, patrolling territories that can stretch for miles. Spotting one means you've connected with the wildness of the forest in its purest form. The jaguar's muscular build, distinctive rosettes on its fur, and intense golden eyes are unforgettable.

Most jaguar sightings happen at dawn or dusk when the cat is most active. Experienced guides know the animal's favorite trails and waterholes, and their trackers use subtle signs — broken branches, paw prints, and scratch marks — to pinpoint potential encounters.

Here's what I learned: patience is everything. Hours can pass with nothing but the sounds of the forest, but when a jaguar finally appears, every second of waiting is worth it. If you want to maximize your chances, plan visits during the dry season, when animals congregate around shrinking water sources.

Monkeys: The Forest's Playful Acrobats

Monkeys are among the most entertaining and visible inhabitants of the Amazon. From the tiny tamarins with their bright orange fur to the curious capuchins and howler monkeys whose calls echo for miles, these primates add a lively soundtrack to the forest.

I recall a moment in Yasuni when a troop of squirrel monkeys passed overhead on a network of vines and branches. Their quick movements and constant chatter made it impossible not to smile. Watching their social interactions — grooming, playing, and communicating — offered a glimpse into the complex social lives of these remarkable creatures.

To see monkeys at their best, early morning treks are ideal. This is when many species are most active, foraging and interacting before the midday heat sets in. Guides often carry binoculars and field guides to help identify different species, enhancing the experience with fascinating facts about behavior and ecology.

Macaws: Colorful Spectacles of the Canopy

No visit to the Amazon is complete without witnessing the breathtaking sight of macaws in flight. Their brilliant reds, blues, and yellows light up the forest canopy like living jewels.

I was lucky enough to visit a clay lick in Manu where macaws gather daily to consume the mineral-rich soil. This behavior is critical for their digestion and detoxification and offers a spectacular opportunity for close observation and photography.

The cacophony of macaws squawking and flapping their wings is both chaotic and mesmerizing. These social birds often travel in flocks, making their presence known from miles away. Birdwatching expeditions targeting macaws often also reveal other spectacular species like toucans and parrots, adding layers of delight to your experience.

Exotic Plants: Nature's Pharmacy and Art Gallery

While the Amazon is renowned for its animals, its botanical wonders are equally astonishing. During my expeditions, I was repeatedly amazed by the incredible diversity and utility of the forest's plant life.

One of the most memorable experiences was learning from indigenous guides about medicinal plants that have been used for centuries. From leaves that reduce inflammation to roots with powerful antiseptic properties, the knowledge passed down is both profound and practical.

The forest is also home to some of the most unusual plants on the planet — towering kapok trees that can reach over 70 meters, orchids with delicate petals in every color imaginable, and giant water lilies whose leaves can support the weight of a small child.

For travelers interested in botany, guided walks with knowledgeable naturalists are invaluable. They help you understand not just what you're seeing, but how plants interact with animals, insects, and the wider ecosystem. This deeper understanding transforms a simple walk into a journey of discovery.

Night Safaris: The Forest After Dark

The Amazon does not sleep when the sun sets — it transforms. Night safaris offer a whole new world of wildlife watching, where nocturnal creatures emerge from their hiding places and the forest bursts with unfamiliar sounds.

I'll never forget my first night walk in Yasuni. Armed with a powerful flashlight and accompanied by an experienced guide, I was both terrified and thrilled. The beam of light revealed glowing eyes of caimans lurking by the river, frogs with vivid markings, and insects that shimmered like jewels.

Night safaris require careful preparation. The terrain is tricky, and many animals are shy or dangerous. Your guide will teach you how to move quietly and spot subtle signs in the dark. Bring long sleeves and pants for protection against insects, and never wander off the trail.

Birdwatching Expeditions: For the Passionate and Curious

If you have even a passing interest in birds, the Amazon's parks are a paradise beyond compare. I spent many early mornings on birdwatching expeditions, feeling the crisp, damp air and listening to the dawn chorus of hundreds of species.

Madidi alone is home to over 1,300 bird species, including the elusive harpy eagle and the dazzling Amazonian umbrellabird. These expeditions are usually led by expert ornithologists or local guides with encyclopedic knowledge of the birds' habits and habitats.

Birdwatching is not just about ticking off species — it's about understanding behaviors, migrations, and the critical role birds play in seed dispersal and pollination. For those willing to wake before dawn, the rewards are endless.

Conservation Efforts: Protecting the Amazon's Future

Behind every amazing wildlife encounter is a story of tireless conservation efforts. These national parks are living laboratories of ecological preservation, but they face relentless threats from deforestation, mining, and climate change.

I was privileged to meet members of indigenous communities who partner with park authorities to protect their ancestral lands. Their knowledge and stewardship are vital to preserving the delicate balance of the rainforest.

Organizations working in these parks focus on scientific research, sustainable tourism, and education programs that empower locals and visitors alike. When you travel responsibly, your presence supports these efforts directly — helping fund anti-poaching patrols, habitat restoration, and community development.

Indigenous Partnerships: Guardians of the Forest

Indigenous peoples have lived in harmony with the Amazon for millennia, and their voices are essential in shaping the future of conservation. During my travels, I witnessed firsthand the strength and wisdom of these partnerships.

In many areas, indigenous guides lead tours, sharing stories that connect visitors to the spiritual and ecological significance of the forest. Their traditional practices — from hunting techniques to medicinal plant use — offer invaluable insights into sustainable living.

Respecting indigenous cultures means listening, learning, and supporting their rights to land and self-determination. This is not just ethical travel — it is essential for the survival of the forest itself.

TREKKING AND RIVER ADVENTURES

Have you ever imagined yourself cutting through thick, damp jungle foliage, the chorus of cicadas and distant bird calls ringing in your ears, the smell of earth and rain heavy around you? Or perhaps gliding silently along a winding river in a canoe, surrounded by towering trees that seem to touch the sky? The Amazon rainforest is not just a place to observe — it is a place to immerse yourself in, to move through, to experience with all your senses.

When I first ventured into this labyrinth of green, my heart raced with anticipation and a touch of nervousness. I had read countless stories, studied maps, and packed my bags with what I thought was everything I'd need. But nothing could prepare me for the electrifying sensation of stepping onto a narrow jungle trail for the first time or pushing a canoe through calm waters at dawn. These are moments when the Amazon reveals itself — wild, unpredictable, and breathtakingly beautiful.

In this chapter, I will share the secrets and insider knowledge gained from my own journeys — the best jungle trails, the must-do river adventures, the safety precautions that could save your life, and the places to rest your head under a canopy of stars. Whether you're a seasoned adventurer or a curious first-timer, this guide will help you navigate the Amazon's challenges and rewards with confidence and respect.

Jungle Trails: Paths Into the Heart of the Forest

Walking through the Amazon jungle is unlike any hike you've done before. The terrain is soft yet uneven, often muddy, and alive with surprises. During my first trek in Manu National Park, the trail was a narrow ribbon weaving through towering trees, vines draped like curtains, and a carpet of fallen leaves and orchids beneath my feet.

The jungle trails here are not just pathways — they are lifelines connecting you to the rhythms of the forest. Every step reveals signs of wildlife:

the fresh tracks of tapirs, the subtle chewed leaves of leafcutter ants, the distant calls of toucans. Your senses sharpen — the air thickens with humidity and the scent of wet wood, the sunlight filters through the canopy in golden shafts, and the symphony of birdsong accompanies you.

Some of the most famous trails are in Madidi National Park, where guided hikes take you from lowland rainforests to cloud forests in just hours. The ecological diversity along these trails is staggering. On one trek, I watched a tiny poison dart frog hop across a leaf, and a few hours later, I was staring up at a majestic Andean condor soaring high above.

If you're considering a jungle trek, here are some essential tips I learned the hard way:

- Wear lightweight, breathable clothing that covers your arms and legs. The jungle is home to many insects, and long sleeves offer protection without overheating.
- Invest in good quality waterproof hiking boots with solid grip. Slipping on muddy slopes is a common hazard.
- Carry a walking stick or trekking pole to steady yourself on uneven terrain and to gently move aside vines or branches.
- Always hike with an experienced local guide. They know the trails, how to read animal signs, and what plants to avoid.
- Bring insect repellent and apply it regularly. Mosquitoes and other biting insects are abundant, especially near water.
- Keep hydrated. Bring plenty of water and use purification tablets or filters if you refill from natural sources.
- Prepare for sudden rain. A lightweight rain jacket or poncho can make all the difference.

Boat Trips: The Amazon from the Water

The rivers of the Amazon are like highways through the forest, providing access to places unreachable by foot. When I boarded a small motorized boat on the Tambopata River, I felt like I was entering a new realm — where water and forest blend seamlessly into one.

Boat trips range from short excursions to multi-day journeys, each offering unique perspectives. On the water, you can observe animals coming to drink or hunt, glimpse pink river dolphins playing, and admire the reflections of giant kapok trees mirrored perfectly in the calm surface.

One unforgettable experience was a dawn boat trip in Yasuni, where the mist hovered just above the river and the forest slowly came to life. The guide pointed out the distinctive nests of weaver birds, the flash of a kingfisher diving, and the haunting call of a hoatzin, a prehistoric bird found only in this region.

If you plan on taking boat trips, remember:

- Wear sun protection — the reflection from the water intensifies sun exposure.
- Bring waterproof bags or cases for your gear, especially electronics.
- Always wear a life jacket when on the water, even if you're a strong swimmer.
- Carry binoculars and a camera with a good zoom to capture distant wildlife.
- Respect speed limits and quiet zones to avoid disturbing wildlife.

Canoeing Routes: Silent Explorations

For the more adventurous, canoeing is a way to slip quietly through the Amazon's intricate waterways, getting closer to wildlife without the noise of motors. I spent several days canoeing in Madidi, navigating narrow tributaries lined with overhanging trees, sometimes paddling alongside flocks of parrots or startled river otters.

Canoeing requires more skill and stamina than boat trips but offers unparalleled intimacy with the environment. The silence allows you to hear subtle sounds — the splash of a fish, the distant howl of monkeys, the rustle of leaves as a capybara moves through the underbrush.

Before you set off on a canoeing adventure, consider these pointers:

- Familiarize yourself with basic paddling techniques and commands. Local guides will give a quick briefing but being comfortable in the canoe helps.
- Pack light and waterproof everything. Canoes have limited storage, and wet gear can ruin your trip.
- Wear a hat and long sleeves to protect from sun and insects, and bring plenty of water.
- Prepare for physical exertion. Paddling for hours in humid conditions is demanding.
- Travel with a guide who knows the river systems and can navigate safely.

Safety Precautions: Respecting the Power of the Jungle

The Amazon is a place of wonder but also of risks. When I first ventured into its depths, I quickly realized that preparation and respect are non-negotiable.

Here are safety essentials based on my personal experience and advice from local experts:

- Never travel alone. Always go with certified local guides who understand the terrain, wildlife, and weather patterns.
- Make sure your guide has a communication device for emergencies.
- Carry a basic first aid kit, including treatments for insect bites, minor cuts, and allergies.
- Be aware of poisonous plants and insects. Avoid touching or eating anything without guidance.
- Watch out for slippery trails and river currents. Move slowly and carefully.
- Follow all park regulations, including restrictions on fires, camping spots, and waste disposal.
- Keep your vaccinations up to date, especially yellow fever and malaria prophylaxis.
- Inform someone outside your group about your itinerary and expected return times.

Camping: Sleeping Under the Canopy

Nothing compares to spending a night deep in the Amazon rainforest. I've camped under a vast canopy where the forest hums with life — the distant calls of howler monkeys, the croaking of frogs, and the rustle of leaves stirred by nocturnal animals.

Many parks offer designated camping areas with basic facilities, but for the truly adventurous, wild camping with a trusted guide is possible. The experience is humbling and magical, connecting you to the forest's heartbeat.

When camping in the Amazon, remember:

- Use a sturdy mosquito net. The jungle is home to many biting insects and disease carriers.
- Bring a lightweight, breathable sleeping bag suitable for warm and humid conditions.
- Pack a compact, portable stove or plan meals with your guide.
- Store food securely to avoid attracting wildlife.
- Keep a flashlight or headlamp handy, plus extra batteries.
- Respect the environment. Leave no trace and follow all park rules.

Eco-Lodges: Comfort Meets Conservation

For those who want immersion without sacrificing comfort, eco-lodges offer an excellent balance. I stayed in several eco-lodges in Yasuni and Manu that blend seamlessly into the environment while providing clean, comfortable accommodation and delicious local food.

Many eco-lodges are run by indigenous communities or conservation organizations, so your stay supports local economies and preservation efforts directly. From solar power and composting toilets to guided nature walks and cultural presentations, these lodges provide an enriching experience.

When choosing an eco-lodge, consider:

- Location and proximity to key park attractions.
- The lodge's commitment to sustainable practices.
- Availability of expert guides and educational programs.
- Guest reviews emphasizing safety and comfort.

CHAPTER 2

ANDES MOUNTAIN PARKS – PEAKS, VOLCANOES, AND GLACIERS

MAJESTIC MOUNTAIN LANDSCAPES

Have you ever stood at the base of a towering peak and felt the sheer scale of the world press in around you? That overwhelming sensation of insignificance — but also pure exhilaration — when the mountains call you closer? The Andes, stretching thousands of kilometers along South America's spine, offer some of the most breathtaking alpine landscapes on the planet. They are a playground of jagged peaks, smoldering volcanoes, and ancient glaciers, each holding stories of natural power and human perseverance.

During my many expeditions through Torres del Paine in Chile, Huascarán in Peru, and Cotopaxi in Ecuador, I have been spellbound by the diversity and drama of these mountain parks. The raw grandeur of sharp granite spires piercing the sky, the roar of glaciers calving into turquoise lakes, and the restless rumblings of volcanic activity create a sensory experience unlike any other. But beyond the awe, there is much to know to explore safely and capture these landscapes in all their majesty.

Let me take you on a journey through these iconic parks, sharing personal stories, practical advice, and expert tips so you can fully embrace the spirit of the Andes — whether you're a climber, a hiker, a photographer, or simply a lover of wild places.

Torres del Paine: Chile's Crown Jewel of the Andes

Imagine a landscape so striking it feels almost otherworldly. That's Torres del Paine National Park — a jewel of Patagonia's southern Andes. The park's namesake, the Torres themselves, are three granite towers soaring sharply into the sky, framed by glaciers, turquoise lakes, and wind-sculpted valleys.

When I first set foot on the W Trek, the most famous trail here, I was engulfed by relentless wind and dazzling light that transformed the scenery with every step. Crossing alpine meadows dotted with lenga trees and glacial rivers rushing beneath ancient ice, I felt simultaneously humbled and alive.

The park's topography is a stunning mix of rugged peaks, deep fjords, and vast glaciers like Grey Glacier — a moving river of ice that cracks and groans as it calves massive chunks into Lake Grey. Guided treks often include boat rides close to the glacier's towering face, an unforgettable sensory overload of cold mist and thunderous icefalls.

Volcanic Activity: Living Landscapes

One of the most thrilling aspects of Andes mountain parks is their volcanic nature. Cotopaxi in Ecuador is one of the world's highest active volcanoes, and standing near its snowy summit is an experience charged with power and respect.

I remember the sheer excitement mixed with nervous energy during a guided ascent of Cotopaxi. The volcano's perfect cone loomed over the valley, a stark contrast to the lush green foothills below. Although the summit hike is challenging, the landscape feels alive — steam vents, sulfuric smells, and the sense that you are standing on the edge of the Earth's molten heart.

Volcanic activity also shapes the landscape in Torres del Paine and Huascarán. For example, volcanic soils support unique ecosystems, and the constant geological activity creates fresh landforms, making every visit dynamic and evolving.

Glacier Exploration: The Slow Sculptors of Stone and Ice

Glaciers in the Andes are living giants, slowly carving the mountains over millennia. Huascarán National Park in Peru offers some of the best glacier trekking opportunities. It was here, standing on a blue ice field with crampons strapped to my boots, that I truly appreciated the glaciers' immense scale and fragile beauty.

Glaciers are deceptive. From afar, they appear serene and solid, but up close, you realize the surface is jagged, crevassed, and shifting. Guided glacier hikes are thrilling and require specialized equipment and knowledge. My guides were invaluable, teaching me how to use ice axes and crampons, read the terrain, and spot hidden dangers.

As climate change accelerates glacier retreat, visiting these ice fields carries a bittersweet awareness — these ancient giants are vanishing. Respecting their power and fragility is part of the experience.

Photography Tips for Alpine Environments

Capturing the Andes' breathtaking landscapes is an art that blends technical skill with creative vision. Over many trips, I've learned several photography secrets that transform ordinary snapshots into stunning alpine portraits.

- Light is everything. In the mountains, the light changes rapidly. Early mornings and late afternoons offer soft, warm tones, while midday sun creates harsh shadows. Plan shoots around these golden hours.
- Use a polarizing filter to reduce glare from snow and water, enhancing colors and contrast.
- Include foreground elements — a wildflower, a rock formation, or a tree branch — to create depth and scale.
- Carry extra batteries and memory cards. Cold temperatures drain batteries faster, so keep spares warm and accessible.
- A tripod is essential for long exposures, especially if you want to capture star trails or silky-smooth waterfalls.

- Don't forget to look up. The sky in the Andes often offers dramatic clouds or brilliant stars that add drama and context to your shots.

Insider Knowledge: Preparing for the Andes

Mountains demand respect and preparation. Here are some insider tips from my journeys to help you stay safe and enjoy every moment:

- Altitude acclimatization is critical. Spend a few days at intermediate elevations before ascending higher to avoid altitude sickness.
- Weather can be unpredictable. Pack layered clothing including waterproof and windproof outerwear.
- Stay hydrated and eat energy-rich foods to maintain stamina.
- Hire local guides who know the terrain intimately and can provide valuable insights.
- Carry a detailed map and GPS device, but also learn to navigate using natural landmarks.
- Respect local regulations and cultural sites.

HIKING AND TREKKING ROUTES

There's a special kind of magic that happens when you lace up your boots at dawn and step onto a trail winding through some of the most spectacular mountains on Earth. The Andes are home to legendary trekking routes that challenge your endurance, ignite your spirit of adventure, and reveal landscapes so stunning they haunt your dreams long after you've returned home.

I remember the first time I tackled the W Trek in Torres del Paine. The biting wind cut through my jacket, the rugged granite spires towered above like ancient sentinels, and every step felt like walking inside a living postcard. Months later, I found myself navigating the remote Huayhuash Circuit in Peru, a high-altitude trek through dramatic peaks and turquoise lakes. And then there was Cotopaxi — standing at the base of that perfect volcanic cone, preparing for a climb that tested every ounce of my stamina and willpower.

Each trek offers something unique, but one thing is certain: preparation, understanding the terrain, and knowing the rules can transform your experience from overwhelming to unforgettable. In this chapter, I'll share everything I've learned from those mountains — from route details and difficulty ratings to permit logistics and the eternal debate between guided and self-guided adventures.

The W Trek: Patagonia's Classic Adventure

No list of Andes treks is complete without the W Trek. It's arguably the most famous hike in South America and a must-do for any mountain lover visiting Chile.

The name "W Trek" comes from the shape of the trail, which weaves through valleys and around iconic landmarks like the Torres del Paine granite towers, French Valley, and Grey Glacier. The trek usually takes five to seven days, covering around 80 kilometers of rugged terrain.

Difficulty and Terrain: The W Trek is moderately difficult. Trails vary from well-maintained paths to steep ascents and descents. Wind is often the biggest challenge here; Patagonia is notorious for fierce gusts that can push even experienced hikers off balance. Expect rocky sections, muddy patches, and occasional river crossings.

Highlights:

- Watching the sunrise light up the Torres del Paine towers
- Exploring the French Valley with its dramatic glacier views
- Witnessing the immense Grey Glacier calving icebergs into the lake

Permits and Logistics: No permit is required to enter Torres del Paine National Park, but park entrance fees apply and must be paid at the visitor centers or online. During peak season (November to March), accommodations and campsites book up quickly, so advance reservations are essential.

Accommodation Options: From backcountry campsites to eco-lodges and refugios (mountain huts), the W Trek offers options for every budget and preference.

My Experience: The first time I did the W Trek, I underestimated the wind. On a particularly gusty morning near the French Valley, I had to brace myself against the storm, holding my trekking poles like anchors. The exhaustion melted away, though, when I reached a viewpoint and saw the glacier gleaming in the distance. It was worth every challenging step.

The Huayhuash Circuit: Peru's Remote Alpine Playground

The Huayhuash Circuit is not for the faint-hearted. Often called the jewel of the Peruvian Andes, this 130-kilometer trek is a high-altitude masterpiece, weaving through towering peaks, deep valleys, and pristine glacial lakes.

Difficulty and Terrain: This trek is strenuous and demands excellent physical fitness. Altitudes range from 3500 to over 5000 meters, with some passes exceeding 4900 meters. The terrain includes rocky trails, scree slopes, and occasional snowfields. Weather can be unpredictable, ranging from intense sun to sudden storms.

Highlights:

- Views of peaks like Yerupajá and Siula Grande, some of the highest in Peru
- Crystal-clear lakes such as Laguna Jahuacocha and Laguna Carhuacocha
- Remote villages where local Quechua culture thrives

Permits and Logistics: No official permit system exists for the Huayhuash Circuit, but trekkers must register with local authorities. Hiring a guide is highly recommended due to the remoteness and complexity of the route.

Accommodation Options: Mostly camping along the trail. Some trekkers opt for basic guesthouses in villages, but the majority is wild camping under the stars.

My Experience: I'll never forget the day I crossed the Punta Cuyoc pass at nearly 5000 meters. The thin air made every breath a labor, and my legs burned fiercely. But when I paused to look around, the sweeping panorama of snow-capped giants was more than a reward — it was a life-affirming moment. The quiet, the vastness, and the knowledge that I was walking a path few had trodden made every grueling step meaningful.

Cotopaxi Climbs: Conquering the Perfect Cone

Cotopaxi Volcano in Ecuador is an icon. Standing at nearly 5900 meters, it is one of the highest active volcanoes in the world. Climbing Cotopaxi is a dream for many, but it demands respect, preparation, and acclimatization.

Difficulty and Terrain: The climb is technically non-technical but challenging due to altitude and icy conditions near the summit. The final sections require crampons and ice axe skills, so mountaineering experience or training is essential.

Highlights:

- The breathtaking views of surrounding peaks from the summit
- The sensation of standing above the clouds
- Observing volcanic activity such as fumaroles and steam vents

Permits and Logistics: Climbing Cotopaxi requires a permit, usually arranged through local guides or agencies. Access is regulated to preserve the environment and ensure safety.

Accommodation Options: Base camps and mountain huts are available near the park entrance. Many climbers stay in Latacunga or Quito the night before the ascent.

My Experience: Standing on Cotopaxi's summit was the pinnacle of my Andean adventures. The cold wind biting at my face, the crunch of ice under my boots, and the panoramic vista stretching endlessly — it was exhilarating and humbling. The climb tested every skill I had, but with a knowledgeable guide by my side, I felt safe and supported.

Difficulty Levels: Matching Your Trek to Your Fitness and Experience

Not all Andes treks are created equal, and understanding the difficulty is key to a successful trip.

- **Easy to Moderate:** The W Trek falls mostly into this category, suitable for hikers with moderate fitness. Trails are well-marked, and support infrastructure is excellent.
- **Strenuous:** The Huayhuash Circuit demands high endurance, acclimatization to altitude, and some backcountry skills. Suitable for experienced trekkers comfortable with long days and rugged terrain.

- **Technical Climbs:** Cotopaxi requires mountaineering skills for its icy summit sections and is recommended only for those with prior experience or who hire certified guides.

Permit Requirements and Regulations

South American mountain parks have varying rules:

- **Torres del Paine:** No permit needed but entrance fee applies.
- **Huayhuash Circuit:** No official permits, but registration with local authorities is mandatory.
- **Cotopaxi:** Climbing permits are required and must be arranged in advance.

In all cases, respecting local regulations protects fragile ecosystems and ensures safety. Always check current rules with official park websites or trusted guides.

Guided vs. Self-Guided Trekking: Pros, Cons, and What's Right for You

Guided Trekking

Hiring a guide or joining a trekking group offers numerous advantages:

- **Safety:** Guides know the trails, weather patterns, and how to handle emergencies.
- **Local Knowledge:** They share insights on flora, fauna, and cultural history.
- **Logistics:** Guides arrange permits, transport, accommodation, and meals.
- **Support:** Carrying heavy gear is often reduced with porters or pack animals.

I've often chosen guided treks in the Andes, especially in remote areas like Huayhuash, where navigation is complex and conditions harsh. The peace of mind and enriched experience are invaluable.

Self-Guided Trekking

For experienced hikers who prefer independence, self-guided trekking offers freedom:

- Set your own pace and schedule.
- Explore less crowded routes or side trails.
- Budget-friendly, as you avoid guide and agency fees.

However, self-guided trekking demands:

- Excellent navigation skills.
- Thorough preparation and contingency planning.
- Ability to manage all logistics independently.

I once attempted a self-guided day hike near Cotopaxi and quickly realized the value of a guide. Trails can be confusing, and weather changes quickly, so I recommend self-guided only if you have significant mountain experience.

Insider Tips for Trekking Success

- Train physically before your trip. Focus on cardio, strength, and endurance.
- Acclimatize properly to avoid altitude sickness — ascending slowly, hydrating, and resting.
- Pack smart: layered clothing, sturdy boots, sun protection, and a good quality backpack.
- Carry a reliable map and GPS device. Download offline maps on your phone.
- Respect the environment: pack out all trash and stick to trails.
- Learn basic first aid and carry a small kit.
- Engage with local communities and support sustainable tourism.

WILDLIFE AND CONSERVATION IN THE ANDES MOUNTAIN PARKS

Have you ever felt that primal thrill of spotting a massive bird soaring effortlessly overhead, its shadow sweeping over a rugged cliff face? Or the rare, electrifying moment when a spectacled bear crosses your path, peering cautiously from dense forest shadows? The Andes are alive with such moments — a living mosaic of extraordinary wildlife, ecosystems at risk, and human efforts to protect these treasures for generations to come.

I've stood breathless on a rocky ridge in Torres del Paine, watching an Andean condor ride thermals high above the valleys. I've trekked across the Peruvian puna, eyes scanning for elusive vicuñas grazing on sparse grass. And deep in Bolivia's remote cloud forests, I once caught a glimpse of the spectacled bear, a shy guardian of the mountains. Each encounter etched itself into my memory — reminders that the Andes are not just landscapes, but vibrant habitats filled with life fighting to endure.

But this wildlife also faces profound threats. Accelerating climate change is melting glaciers that sustain fragile ecosystems. Human activity pressures habitats and wildlife populations. National parks are frontline defenders, balancing visitor access with conservation imperatives. Let me share with you a deep dive into the iconic animals, the urgent environmental challenges, and how you can travel responsibly to support these mountain sanctuaries.

Majestic Andean Condors: Kings of the Sky

There are few sights as awe-inspiring as the silhouette of an Andean condor against the vast mountain sky. With wingspans reaching nearly three meters, these birds are the largest flying land birds in the world. Watching one effortlessly soar over rugged cliffs and sweeping valleys is like witnessing a living symbol of the Andes' wild spirit.

I recall a dawn hike near the Torres del Paine massif when suddenly, a condor appeared, circling lazily on thermals, riding the rising warm air currents. The bird's keen eyes surveyed the landscape below as it gracefully glided — an ancient presence dating back millions of years.

Ecological Role: Condors are scavengers, cleaning up carrion and preventing disease spread. Their role is vital for ecosystem health.

Threats: Despite their majesty, condors face threats from habitat loss, poisoning, and collisions with power lines. Conservation programs in Chile, Peru, and Ecuador have focused on captive breeding and reintroduction with encouraging success.

Viewing Tips: Early mornings and late afternoons are best for spotting condors near cliffs and valleys. National parks often have designated viewpoints. Use binoculars and avoid sudden movements to prevent disturbance.

Vicuñas: The High-Altitude Wool Collectors

Vicuñas are delicate cousins of llamas, famed for their ultra-fine wool that has been treasured since Incan times. These graceful animals roam the high Andean puna grasslands, blending almost invisibly into the golden landscape.

During a hike across Huascarán National Park, I was struck by the elegance of a small herd grazing quietly. Their slender necks and alert eyes epitomize the fragile balance of life at 4000 meters above sea level.

Conservation Success Story: Vicuñas were once hunted nearly to extinction for their valuable fleece. Thanks to strict protection and community-led sustainable harvesting programs, populations have rebounded impressively.

Behavior: Vicuñas are shy and fast, usually fleeing at the first sign of humans. Approach slowly and quietly to observe.

Ecological Importance: As grazers, vicuñas help maintain the grassland ecosystem, preventing overgrowth and supporting biodiversity.

Spectacled Bears: Andean Forest Guardians

The spectacled bear, or Andean bear, is South America's only bear species and one of the most elusive mammals in the Andes. Named for the distinctive markings around their eyes, these bears dwell mainly in cloud forests and high-altitude scrublands.

My most memorable wildlife encounter was deep in Bolivia's Madidi National Park when I glimpsed a spectacled bear foraging among dense bamboo. The bear froze, studied me with intelligent eyes, then disappeared silently into the shadows — a fleeting but unforgettable moment.

Behavior: Mostly solitary and shy, spectacled bears feed on fruits, bromeliads, and occasionally small mammals. They are crucial seed dispersers, helping regenerate forest ecosystems.

Conservation Challenges: Habitat loss from agriculture and mining poses severe threats. Additionally, conflicts with local farmers sometimes lead to persecution.

Conservation Efforts: Protected areas like Madidi are key refuges. Community education programs aim to reduce human-wildlife conflicts and promote coexistence.

Glacial Retreat and Climate Impact: A Crisis Unfolding

The Andes are home to some of the world's most significant tropical glaciers, essential for regional water supply, agriculture, and ecological balance. Yet these glaciers are retreating at an alarming rate due to rising global temperatures.

During a visit to Huascarán National Park, I witnessed firsthand the dramatic retreat of ice fields that once dominated the landscape. Lakes have expanded, new vegetation has colonized exposed rock, and watercourses have shifted. While this is a natural process, the speed of change today is unprecedented and troubling.

Implications:

- **Water Security:** Millions depend on glacier-fed rivers for drinking water and irrigation.
- **Biodiversity:** Changing water regimes disrupt habitats and species' survival.
- **Natural Hazards:** Melting glaciers increase risks of glacial lake outburst floods.

Scientific Monitoring: Many parks collaborate with scientists using satellite imagery and field studies to track glacial health and inform conservation strategies.

Park Management: Balancing Tourism and Preservation

Effective management is the backbone of conserving the Andes' fragile mountain ecosystems. National parks like Torres del Paine, Huascarán, Cotopaxi, and Madidi have developed strategies to protect wildlife and habitats while welcoming visitors.

Key Elements:

- **Visitor Limits:** Many parks regulate daily visitor numbers during peak seasons to reduce environmental impact.
- **Zoning:** Sensitive areas are often off-limits or restricted to guided tours only.
- **Waste Management:** Strict "pack-in, pack-out" policies minimize pollution.
- **Community Involvement:** Indigenous groups are engaged in co-managing parks, blending traditional knowledge with modern conservation.
- **Education:** Visitor centers and interpretive trails provide vital information on wildlife and responsible behavior.

Visitor Guidelines: Respecting Nature and Culture

As a traveler, your actions can profoundly impact these protected landscapes. When visiting Andes mountain parks, keep these principles in mind:

- **Keep Distance:** Always observe wildlife from a safe distance to avoid stress or behavioral changes.
- **Stay on Trails:** Protect fragile vegetation and prevent erosion by sticking to marked paths.
- **No Feeding:** Feeding wildlife alters their natural habits and can cause harm.
- **Leave No Trace:** Pack out all trash and avoid leaving any impact behind.
- **Respect Cultural Sites:** Many parks encompass indigenous sacred sites; honor local customs and restrictions.
- **Use Eco-Friendly Products:** Choose biodegradable soaps and avoid single-use plastics.

Personal Reflection: The Call to Protect

Every wildlife encounter in the Andes has reinforced my conviction that conservation is not optional — it is essential. The Andean condor's soaring flight, the vicuña's gentle grace, the spectacled bear's wary glance — these moments remind me that we share this planet with beings whose survival depends on our choices.

Climate change, habitat destruction, and human pressures threaten these mountain sanctuaries more than ever. But hope lies in the passionate work of park managers, local communities, scientists, and responsible travelers.

When I return to these wild places, I do so with renewed gratitude and a fierce commitment to tread lightly and advocate for their protection. The Andes will endure if we choose to respect and protect them.

CHAPTER 3

PATAGONIA NATIONAL PARKS – WINDSWEPT WILDERNESS AND FJORDS

ICONIC FJORDS AND GLACIAL LANDSCAPES

Imagine standing at the edge of a massive glacier, the air crackling with an icy chill, the vastness of ancient ice stretching as far as your eyes can see. Now imagine the wind whipping fiercely across your face, carrying with it the salty scent of fjord waters that have carved the landscape over millennia. This is Patagonia: a raw, untamed wilderness where glaciers dominate, fjords weave deep into the coastline, and every vista is a masterpiece of nature's most dramatic artistry.

If you've ever dreamed of exploring these wild lands, let me assure you—your excitement will be matched only by the intensity of the experience. I've been there, countless times, caught in the sweep of Patagonia's windstorms, mesmerized by the thunderous calving of glaciers, and humbled by the vast, silent beauty of Los Glaciares National Park in Argentina and Torres del Paine National Park in Chile. Each journey into these parks is a visceral encounter with Earth's elemental forces.

But it's not just about awe. To truly appreciate Patagonia, you need insider knowledge—when to go, how to navigate its rugged fjords, which boat tours offer the best access, and how to prepare for the unpredictable weather that reigns over this land. That's exactly what this section will deliver: a precise, exhilarating guide infused with personal stories, practical tips, and expert advice to make your Patagonian adventure unforgettable.

Los Glaciares National Park: The Argentine Ice Giant

The first time I laid eyes on the Perito Moreno Glacier in Los Glaciares National Park, I was utterly overwhelmed. Standing at the viewing platform, the glacier's colossal face stretched over 60 meters high above the lake, a wall of shimmering blue ice cracked with deep crevices. Every few minutes, the glacier groaned and fractured with a deafening crack, sending colossal chunks of ice crashing into the emerald water below. The sound reverberated in my chest—it was a natural symphony of power and fragility that no picture can capture.

Why Los Glaciares? This park holds some of the most accessible and dynamic glaciers in the world, making it an essential destination for anyone seeking the rawness of ice and mountain wilderness. Unlike many glaciers that are quietly receding, Perito Moreno is one of the few that remains stable or even advancing, creating constant movement and spectacular ice calving events.

Exploring the Glacier: The park offers multiple ways to experience the glacier. I highly recommend combining these three approaches for the fullest experience:

- **Viewing Platforms:** Well-maintained walkways and observation decks provide jaw-dropping panoramas of Perito Moreno.

Visiting in the early morning or late afternoon lets you catch the ice in varying light, adding depth and drama to the glacier's textures.

- **Boat Tours:** One of my favorite moments was cruising close to the glacier's face aboard a small boat. The sheer scale becomes humbling when you realize that the icy cliffs tower above you, their deep blue hues shifting with every crack and wave. These boat tours depart from Puerto Bajo de las Sombras and glide across Lago Argentino, offering unique perspectives.
- **Ice Trekking:** For the ultimate adventure, guided ice trekking allows you to walk on the glacier itself. Wearing crampons and harnesses, you explore ice caves, deep crevasses, and rugged ridges under the guidance of experienced guides. It's physically demanding but one of the most thrilling outdoor activities I've ever done.

Scenic Drives: The drive to Los Glaciares from El Calafate is an adventure in itself. Winding roads pass through Patagonian steppe dotted with guanacos and lenga forests. The expansive landscape shifts from flat plains to rolling hills, setting the tone for what's to come. Insider tip: stop at viewpoints along Ruta 11 to snap photos of the shimmering lakes that reflect the distant ice fields.

Torres del Paine National Park: Chile's Crown Jewel

Crossing into Chile, Torres del Paine offers a strikingly different but equally breathtaking experience. Known worldwide for its jagged peaks, turquoise lakes, and windswept plains, this park epitomizes Patagonian wilderness. When I first arrived at the park entrance, the wind immediately reminded me that this place demands respect—it's untamed, unpredictable, and endlessly beautiful.

Iconic Fjords and Glaciers: Unlike Los Glaciares, Torres del Paine's glaciers are part of a massive ice field, the Southern Patagonian Ice Field, the world's second-largest contiguous extrapolar ice mass. The Grey Glacier, a spectacular arm of this ice field, flows into the fjord-like Grey Lake, offering dramatic contrasts of blue ice against dark waters and rugged mountain peaks.

Boat Tours: I took a memorable boat tour across Grey Lake, where the silence was punctuated only by the occasional crack of ice breaking off the glacier. The captain skillfully navigated close to the glacier front, giving us a close-up view of towering ice cliffs. Watching giant icebergs drift past, some polished and translucent, others jagged and opaque, felt like witnessing a primordial dance frozen in time.

Scenic Drives and Sightseeing: The park's road network is surprisingly well-developed for such a remote area, allowing access to key viewpoints like Salto Grande waterfall, Lago Nordenskjöld, and the base of the Torres del Paine peaks.

I highly recommend stopping often; every bend reveals new panoramas that defy expectation.

Hiking Options: While this chapter focuses on fjords and glaciers, I can't help but mention the iconic W Trek trails near these water bodies. The balance of rugged mountains, icy water, and Patagonian steppe creates hiking vistas that remain etched in memory.

Boat Tours: The Best Way to Experience Patagonia's Fjords and Ice

If you want to connect intimately with Patagonia's glacial landscapes, boat tours are indispensable. Whether in Argentina's Lago Argentino or Chile's Grey Lake, being on the water gives you perspectives and sensations no land-based viewpoint can.

Choosing Your Boat Tour: Not all tours are created equal. When I researched options, I found that the best tours balance proximity to glaciers, safety, and environmental responsibility. For example, some operators maintain small groups and use eco-friendly boats to minimize disturbance.

What to Expect: Patagonian waters are cold and often choppy. Dress in layers with waterproof outerwear and bring gloves and hats. Even on calm days, the wind chill is powerful. The thrill of hearing the glacier crack or ice fall is electrifying and sometimes unnerving.

Photography Tips: Use a polarizing filter to reduce glare on the water and enhance colors. Bring a telephoto lens to capture detailed ice formations and wildlife such as cormorants or Andean geese that often follow the boats.

Insider Secret: Try to book tours during shoulder seasons, like late spring or early fall. The crowds thin out, and you often have the boat almost to yourself.

Glaciers: Understanding Their Majesty and Movement

Patagonia's glaciers are dynamic, living giants. When I first studied glaciology on the trail, I was fascinated by how these massive ice rivers form, flow, and sculpt the landscape.

How Glaciers Form: Snow accumulates over centuries, compressing into dense ice that slowly moves downhill under gravity's pull. Along the way, glaciers carve valleys, polish rock faces, and transport debris.

Calving: The spectacular breaking off of ice chunks into lakes or fjords is called calving. Hearing and seeing this in person is unforgettable. You'll often see huge waves ripple outward as giant blocks crash into the water.

Climate Change Impacts: While Perito Moreno remains stable, many Patagonian glaciers are retreating rapidly. This retreat affects local water cycles and ecosystems. It adds urgency to responsible tourism and conservation efforts.

Seasonal Weather and Best Visiting Times: Planning for the Perfect Patagonian Experience

Patagonia's weather is notoriously unpredictable. I learned this the hard way on my first trip when a sunny morning suddenly turned into a hailstorm within minutes.

Seasons:

- **Summer (December to February):** The most popular season with long daylight hours and milder temperatures. Expect crowds, especially in January.
- **Shoulder Seasons (October to November and March to April):** Cooler but less crowded. Spring brings blooming flora, while fall offers brilliant foliage and golden light.
- **Winter (May to September):** Harsh, cold, and many facilities close. Not recommended for casual travelers but perfect for winter sports enthusiasts.

Weather Tips:

- Dress in layers to adapt quickly to changing conditions.
- Carry waterproof gear and sturdy boots.
- Be prepared for strong winds, often exceeding 100 kilometers per hour.
- Always check local forecasts daily and heed ranger advice.

Best Time to Visit: For a balance of good weather, fewer crowds, and accessible services, I recommend early November or late March. These months offer stunning landscapes, manageable temperatures, and the chance to see wildlife like guanacos and birds in vibrant activity.

Personal Reflections: The Emotional Power of Patagonia's Fjords and Glaciers

Every visit to Patagonia's fjords and glaciers has been a profound reminder of nature's power and fragility. The first time I watched an enormous ice block detach and crash into the water, the vibration rattled my bones and stirred a deep reverence. It felt like witnessing the heartbeat of the planet itself.

I've stood on boat decks, wind tearing at my jacket, camera poised, heart pounding, knowing that moments like this define why we travel. Patagonia doesn't just show you beautiful scenes — it changes how you see the world.

ADVENTURE HIKING AND CAMPING IN PATAGONIA NATIONAL PARKS

Circuit Trails, Base Camps, and Refuge Systems

If you ever wondered what it feels like to be completely swallowed by the vastness of Patagonia, to hear only the wind and the crunch of your boots on gravel, to wake up surrounded by peaks carved by glaciers millions of years ago — then adventure hiking and camping here is the answer. I still recall the overwhelming thrill I felt the moment I stepped onto the W Circuit trail in Torres del Paine. The sensation was a cocktail of awe, anticipation, and pure adrenaline. I was about to spend days trekking through some of the most spectacular wilderness on Earth, and the experience changed me forever.

Circuit Trails — Pathways to the Heart of Patagonia

Patagonia's network of trekking circuits is world-renowned, with routes that meander past glaciers, turquoise lakes, dense forests, and rugged mountain terrain. The W Circuit and the longer O Circuit in Torres del Paine are perhaps the most famous. In Los Glaciares National Park, the Fitz Roy and Huemul Circuits offer equally stunning challenges.

The W Circuit

I remember starting the W early one brisk morning. The trail lives up to every bit of its reputation — from the dramatic granite spires of the Torres themselves to the sprawling views of glaciers and pristine lakes. Each day brings new terrain and breathtaking scenery, but also real challenges. Winds whip mercilessly, and some sections skirt precarious cliffs or slippery river crossings. It's not a stroll in the park.

The W Circuit is about 80 kilometers, usually completed in four to five days. The route hits key highlights: the Base of the Towers, French Valley, and Grey Glacier. Each campsite and refuge along the way offers basic but comfortable shelter, allowing hikers to recharge.

The O Circuit

For those craving even more adventure and solitude, the O Circuit wraps around the entire Torres del Paine massif. At roughly 130 kilometers and taking 7 to 9 days, it demands serious stamina and preparation. The trail's remoteness means fewer hikers and a deeper connection to Patagonia's wilderness. I was fortunate to tackle the O on a trip that tested both my physical limits and mental grit. Facing unpredictable weather and wild landscapes day after day, I learned how rewarding—and humbling—true wilderness trekking can be.

Fitz Roy and Huemul Circuits

In Argentina's Los Glaciares National Park, the Fitz Roy Circuit encircles the iconic peaks of Mount Fitz Roy and Cerro Torre. These trails pass through lenga forests, glacial valleys, and alpine meadows. The Huemul Circuit is more challenging and less traveled, weaving through pristine landscapes around Lake Argentino's western shore.

Base Camps and Refuge Systems: Finding Your Home in the Wilderness

For anyone new to Patagonian hiking, the refuge system is a godsend. These mountain huts provide shelter, meals, and often a touch of comfort in an otherwise wild environment. I recall arriving at Refugio Paine Grande after a long day's hike, greeted by warm soups, cozy bunks, and fellow adventurers swapping stories around the communal table. It was a moment of camaraderie and rest before the next day's trek.

Most refugios operate on a reservation system, and in high season, they fill quickly. Booking early is crucial. For independent hikers, campsites with tent pads are also available near refugios and along major trails. If you're camping, be prepared for strong winds and cold nights. The best campsites often offer spectacular views but come with the reality of exposed terrain.

The balance between refugios and camping allows trekkers to customize their experience: luxury refugio stays or rugged, self-supported wilderness nights.

Safety Tips and Gear Recommendations: Preparing for the Unexpected

Patagonia is breathtaking but unforgiving. The region's famous winds can blow at 80 to 120 kilometers per hour, and weather can swing from sun to snow in minutes. When I first set out on the trails, I underestimated the conditions and quickly learned that preparation is everything.

Essential Gear

- **Layered Clothing:** Bring moisture-wicking base layers, insulating mid-layers, and a high-quality waterproof and windproof outer shell. I've learned the hard way that a Gore-Tex jacket can be a lifesaver.
- **Footwear:** Sturdy, waterproof hiking boots with good ankle support are mandatory. I used boots with Vibram soles that gripped slippery rocks even in wet conditions.
- **Backpack:** A comfortable pack with a capacity of 50 to 65 liters works well for multi-day hikes, allowing room for gear, food, and extra layers.
- **Sleeping System:** A four-season sleeping bag rated for below freezing temperatures is essential. Combine this with a quality insulated sleeping pad to protect from the cold ground.
- **Trekking Poles:** These are indispensable on steep ascents and descents, helping preserve your knees and improve balance.
- **Navigation Tools:** Even on well-marked trails, I always carry a GPS device, maps, and a compass. Electronics can fail, so redundancy is key.

- **Food and Water:** Carry high-energy snacks like nuts, dried fruits, and energy bars. For water, always use a reliable filtration system—stream water looks pristine but can harbor parasites.
- **Emergency Equipment:** A basic first aid kit, headlamp with extra batteries, whistle, and multi-tool are non-negotiable.

Safety Tips

- **Weather Vigilance:** Always check local weather forecasts and monitor sky conditions during hikes. Patagonian weather is famously changeable.
- **Stick to the Trails:** This is critical for your safety and to preserve fragile ecosystems. Wandering off-trail can lead to injury and environmental damage.
- **Inform Others:** Let park rangers or your accommodation know your itinerary. Communication is limited in remote areas, so leave a detailed plan.
- **Acclimatization:** Although elevations are moderate, the physical demand and cold can affect your performance. Take it slow at first, hydrate well, and listen to your body.
- **Group Travel:** Hiking with others is safer and more enjoyable. If you're solo, be extra cautious and consider hiring a local guide.

Ranger-Led Programs and Wilderness Skills

One of the most rewarding aspects of hiking in Patagonia is the opportunity to learn from the experts—park rangers and experienced guides who live and breathe the land. During my trips, I participated in several ranger-led programs that deepened my understanding of Patagonian ecosystems, wildlife, and survival skills.

Programs Available

Rangers often host educational talks on the park's geology, flora, and fauna. Some parks offer guided walks that teach hikers how to identify native plants or track wildlife footprints. For those interested in wilderness skills, workshops on navigation, first aid, and Leave No Trace principles are available.

I vividly remember a session where a ranger showed our group how to set up a wind-resistant camp in exposed locations—a critical skill given Patagonia's relentless gusts. Learning to pitch a tent anchored firmly with rocks and tying guy lines correctly can mean the difference between a restful night and a miserable ordeal.

Wilderness Skills to Master

- **Map and Compass Navigation:** GPS devices are helpful but should never replace fundamental navigation skills. Understanding topography, reading contour lines, and using a compass remain crucial.
- **Weather Reading:** Rangers teach how to read cloud formations, wind direction, and atmospheric changes to anticipate weather shifts.
- **Wildlife Awareness:** Knowing which animals are present, how to avoid conflicts, and how to respect their habitats ensures both your safety and theirs.
- **Fire Safety:** Open fires are prohibited in many areas to protect the fragile environment. Learning how to cook with stoves safely is essential.
- **Leave No Trace Ethics:** Minimizing your footprint preserves Patagonia's wildness for generations. Rangers emphasize packing out all waste, avoiding trail widening, and respecting flora.

My Personal Journey: Lessons Learned on the Trails

I recall a particular night camping near Lake Nordenskjöld when the wind howled so fiercely I feared my tent would collapse. I had underestimated the strength of Patagonian storms. Battling sleep deprivation, I learned the importance of sturdy gear and patience. That night was a turning point; I came to respect the mountains not just as scenic backdrops but as formidable forces demanding humility and preparation.

Another unforgettable moment came during the O Circuit when a ranger led our group on a navigation workshop. We practiced using map and compass to reroute a trail that had been closed due to flooding. That exercise boosted my confidence and deepened my connection to the landscape.

FLORA, FAUNA, AND ECOSYSTEM PROTECTION

If you ever find yourself standing in the middle of a Patagonian steppe, beneath the endless sky, with nothing but the sharp wind and the scent of earth and grass around you, you'll begin to grasp what real wilderness feels like. I was there before—on a crisp, early morning, watching a small herd of guanacos graze in the golden light. Theirs is not just a story of survival; it's the living pulse of Patagonia's ecosystem.

Understanding this landscape means embracing the fragile, intricate web that supports it—from the smallest moss to the elusive puma stalking the shadows.

Guanacos, Pumas, and Native Flora: The Wild Heart of Patagonia

Let me be brutally honest: Patagonia's wildlife isn't like your typical zoo encounter or even your average national park fauna. This is **raw, undisturbed nature**, and it operates on a clock and scale far older than us.

Guanacos: The Graceful Guardians of the Steppe

Guanacos are the most visible large mammals here, but don't mistake their serene grazing for docility. Watching them for hours, I came to appreciate their hyper-alertness—the way a single guanaco will freeze mid-step, scanning the horizon, ears twitching for the slightest hint of danger. They're not just prey; they are **survivors**, perfectly adapted to withstand Patagonia's brutal winters and fierce winds.

Insider's knowledge? Guanacos are the wild relatives of domesticated llamas, and they form tight family groups. They roam the open grasslands and foothills, controlling vegetation through their grazing habits and acting as prey for apex predators, mainly pumas. Observing a guanaco herd taught me more about social structures in the wild than any textbook.

Pumas: The Silent Apex Predator

If you're lucky—or unlucky—you might catch a glimpse of a puma. These cats are the **ghosts of Patagonia**, rare and elusive. My personal experience hunting for signs of pumas was a lesson in humility. I tracked footprints in mud, scanned distant ridges for movement, and learned how to read their hunting patterns.

Pumas play a crucial role in maintaining balance by regulating herbivore populations like guanacos and red deer. Without them, the ecosystem risks collapse. The sad truth is that pumas face threats from hunting and habitat loss. Conservationists are fighting hard to protect these majestic creatures, and every visitor has a role in supporting their survival.

Native Flora: The Quiet Backbone of the Ecosystem

Patagonia's plant life may not be as immediately striking as its glaciers or mountains, but it is no less vital. I was surprised at how diverse and tough the native flora is. From **coihue trees** in the forested areas to the cushion plants that carpet the windswept plains, these species have evolved to survive extreme conditions of wind, cold, and nutrient-poor soils.

Many plants have deep roots that stabilize the soil and prevent erosion. Others have special adaptations to conserve water and nutrients. I spent a day with a local botanist who showed me how even the smallest mosses and lichens contribute to carbon sequestration and soil fertility. This is nature's quiet work, underpinning everything you see above ground.

Conservation Programs and Ecological Monitoring: Protecting Patagonia's Future

If you only take one thing away from this chapter, it should be this: **Patagonia's wilderness is fragile, and its protection is a complex, ongoing battle.**

Governments, NGOs, indigenous communities, and scientists have united here in a way I have rarely seen elsewhere. It's a multi-layered effort involving conservation programs that blend traditional knowledge with cutting-edge science.

Ecological Monitoring: The Eyes on the Land

I once spent time with a team of researchers who hike the parks daily, collecting data on wildlife populations, vegetation changes, and climate impact.

They use drones, GPS collars, and even camera traps hidden in the bushes to monitor elusive animals like the endangered huemul deer and the pumas.

Their work is painstaking but vital. I was privileged to witness how data from these programs helps park management make informed decisions about hunting regulations, fire management, and visitor access. The level of dedication blew me away—these are not just scientists; they are **guardians of the wild**.

Community-Led Conservation Initiatives

What struck me most was how the local communities are involved. Many programs support indigenous groups whose ancestral knowledge of the land spans centuries. This partnership is essential because protecting an ecosystem isn't just about preserving species—it's about maintaining the cultural and ecological tapestry that defines Patagonia.

I had an unforgettable conversation with a Mapuche elder who spoke passionately about the connection between their people and the land. He reminded me that conservation here is not just science; it is spirituality, identity, and survival.

Visitor Education and Support for Conservation

Every visitor to Patagonia is a steward by default. Programs that educate tourists on responsible behavior are growing, from mandatory briefings at park entrances to interactive exhibits in visitor centers.

I've seen firsthand how these programs reduce littering, prevent trail erosion, and minimize human-wildlife conflict. For example, visitors learn not to approach or feed wildlife, to stick to marked paths, and to carry out all waste.

Visitor Impact Minimization: How to Tread Lightly in Patagonia

This is where your personal responsibility becomes crucial. I can't emphasize enough how easily visitor pressure can degrade these pristine ecosystems.

Stick to Designated Trails

I once encountered a group that had strayed off trail, crushing fragile cushion plants that took decades to grow. It was heartbreaking. Trails exist to **protect both you and the environment**. Wandering off-track may seem adventurous, but it can cause irreversible damage.

Carry Out All Waste

Even biodegradable waste, like apple cores, can disrupt local wildlife. I carry a small pack for waste on every hike, and I encourage every traveler to do the same. If you don't want to carry it, don't bring it.

Avoid Feeding or Approaching Wildlife

Feeding animals disrupts their natural foraging behavior and can lead to dangerous habituation. In one instance, I saw a guanaco approach humans expecting food—something that should never happen.

Respect Campfire Restrictions

Fire is a major threat in dry conditions. Always use designated fire pits if fires are allowed at all, and follow all guidelines. I've participated in fire prevention campaigns that save hectares of wilderness each year.

Use Eco-Friendly Products

From sunscreen to toiletries, make sure your products do not pollute streams or soil. I carry biodegradable soap and encourage fellow hikers to do the same.

CHAPTER 4

PANTANAL AND WETLANDS – WILDLIFE PARADISE

When I first set foot in the Pantanal, I knew instantly this wasn't just another nature reserve. This was *the* wilderness to experience, a true wildlife paradise that rewrites what you thought you knew about wetlands and biodiversity. I've been there before, navigating the maze of waterways, eyes peeled for elusive creatures, heart pounding with the thrill of the wild. The Pantanal and Esteros del Ibará are not just places; they are living, breathing worlds pulsing with life, color, and raw energy.

WETLAND ECOSYSTEMS AND BIODIVERSITY

The Pantanal in Brazil is the largest tropical wetland on Earth. And just a few hundred miles south, Esteros del Ibará in Argentina offers a complementary ecosystem that, while smaller, is equally stunning. Together, they form a patchwork of lakes, marshes, flooded forests, and savannas that sustain one of the richest biodiversities on the planet.

The Pulse of Water

What struck me immediately, firsthand, was the *rhythm* of the wetlands. These landscapes are defined by the **seasonal flooding**, a natural cycle that transforms dry savannas into vast aquatic corridors. The flooding is no accident; it's a vital pulse that renews life, flushes nutrients, and shapes habitats.

From June to October, the dry season allows you to access roads and trails that become impassable in the rainier months. But when the rains come, usually from November through April, the waters rise, sometimes submerging vast areas for months. This flood pulse drives the entire ecosystem — fish migrate to spawn, birds arrive in great numbers, and mammals adapt their movement and feeding patterns to the changing landscape.

Biodiversity in Action

I remember the first time I spotted a jaguar slipping through the tall grass at the edge of a lagoon, nearly invisible but utterly regal. The Pantanal is a stronghold for jaguars, and seeing one in the wild is a moment I will never forget. But the wildlife spectacle doesn't stop there.

The wetlands are home to:

- Over 650 bird species, including the iconic **hyacinth macaw**, **herons**, and **jabiru stork**.
- Dozens of fish species that form the base of the food web.
- Large mammals like **capybaras**, **giant otters**, and **marsh deer**.
- Reptiles including **caimans** and **anacondas**.
- Countless insects and amphibians that keep the system humming.

During my time exploring these wetlands, I learned from local guides who know these ecosystems intimately. Their stories of animal behavior, migration patterns, and survival strategies brought the wetlands alive in ways no textbook could.

Pantanal (Brazil) and Esteros del Iberá (Argentina)

Pantanal: The Crown Jewel of Brazilian Wetlands

Pantanal is a vast expanse of wetlands covering over 150,000 square kilometers. I was there before, cruising on a wooden boat through dense reeds, the sound of wildlife punctuating the silence. The scale is breathtaking—never-ending floodplains stretching to the horizon, intersected by winding rivers and lagoons.

The Pantanal's biodiversity is the result of its position at the confluence of three major South American river basins: the Paraguay, the Paraná, and the São Francisco. This convergence creates an unparalleled wetland habitat.

Local ranches, called **fazendas**, often double as eco-lodges, blending traditional cattle ranching with conservation efforts. I stayed on one such fazenda where the owners worked with biologists to protect the jaguar population and restore native vegetation. Their approach is a model for sustainable tourism.

Esteros del Iberá: Argentina's Hidden Wetland Treasure

South of the Pantanal, in Argentina's Corrientes province, lies the Esteros del Iberá, a wetland that many travelers overlook but is no less spectacular. The Iberá is smaller but boasts a mosaic of freshwater lagoons, marshes, and flooded grasslands.

I ventured here during the dry season, when the landscape reveals vast expanses of reed beds and shimmering water bodies that reflect the sky. Boat safaris glide silently through channels, revealing species that have become rare elsewhere, including the elusive maned wolf and the curious capuchin monkeys.

The Esteros is an inspiring success story in conservation. Where once overhunting and habitat loss threatened species, dedicated restoration projects and local involvement have helped populations rebound.

Seasonal Flooding and Water-Based Habitats

There's no overstating how central **seasonal flooding** is to the ecology of both the Pantanal and Esteros del Iberá. It's the master architect of the landscape and life cycles.

When the rains swell the rivers, the wetlands expand dramatically. Lakes and ponds swell, terrestrial plants are submerged, and fish access new feeding and breeding grounds. During this time, animals exhibit remarkable adaptability. Fish jump in abundance, birds nest in the flooded trees, and capybaras retreat to higher ground.

When I experienced this seasonal flux firsthand, I was fascinated by the *dynamic* nature of the ecosystem. Unlike static forests or deserts, these wetlands are in constant motion. They demand that animals be resilient and flexible—qualities I witnessed repeatedly while on boat safaris.

Water-Based Habitats and Their Unique Ecology

The wetlands encompass a variety of aquatic habitats, from open lagoons to dense floating vegetation mats. These provide critical breeding grounds for fish and amphibians and feeding areas for migratory birds.

One insider's insight I learned is how the interplay between water and land shapes species diversity. For example, caimans sun themselves on floating logs during the day but disappear beneath the water at the slightest noise. Giant otters use their webbed feet and streamlined bodies to hunt fish in these channels with incredible speed and precision.

Understanding this aquatic connection is key to truly appreciating wetland conservation. The health of the water is the health of the entire ecosystem.

Scenic Drives and Boat Safaris: Immersive Wildlife Experiences

If you're looking for authentic immersion in wetland wilderness, scenic drives and boat safaris are your golden ticket. I was there before, steering through muddy tracks or drifting silently along labyrinthine waterways, and I can say with certainty there's nothing like it.

Scenic Drives: The Road Less Traveled

During the dry season, the Pantanal's dirt roads become accessible, offering incredible opportunities to spot wildlife on land. My advice? Rent a sturdy 4x4 or join guided tours with experienced local drivers who know where to find elusive animals.

From dawn to dusk, the drive is a masterclass in patience and observation. The key is to move slowly, scanning water edges and grasslands for movement. Capybaras and caimans often lounge near the roads, while birds such as the toucan and the vibrant rhea roam freely.

I remember a particularly magical afternoon when my guide stopped the truck near a shallow lagoon, and we watched a family of giant otters playfully fishing. Moments like these are what make the wetland so irresistible.

Boat Safaris: Glide into the Heart of the Wetlands

Boat safaris are the ultimate wetland adventure. There's an unparalleled silence when you glide along the water, punctuated only by birdsong and the splash of fish. The chance to get close to aquatic wildlife, like caimans resting on banks or elusive jaguars hunting near water, is exhilarating.

I recommend choosing small, eco-friendly boats with experienced naturalist guides. Their *insiders' knowledge* of animal habits and habitats can reveal wonders that casual observers miss.

Safety tip: always listen carefully to guides, especially regarding water safety and wildlife behavior. The wetlands are beautiful but can be unpredictable.

WILDLIFE WATCHING OPPORTUNITIES

If you want to understand what it means to *truly* connect with wildlife, you must step into the wetlands of the Pantanal or Esteros del Iberá with patience, respect, and an open heart. I was there before, eyes locked on the subtle signs of life, senses sharpened by countless hours of observation, and a burning excitement coursing through me every time a jaguar's silhouette appeared against the dense foliage or a flock of brilliantly plumed birds erupted from the reeds.

Wildlife watching here is not about ticking boxes or rushing from one sighting to the next. It's about becoming a silent participant in a living tapestry—learning to read the landscape, the behaviors, and the rhythms that govern these creatures' lives. The rewards? Nothing less than breathtaking moments that stay with you forever.

Jaguars, Capybaras, Giant Otters, and Caimans: The Pantanal's Signature Wildlife

Jaguars — The Elusive Kings of the Wetlands

If there is a single species that defines the Pantanal, it's the jaguar. My excitement the first time I caught sight of this magnificent cat was impossible to overstate. Jaguars are the apex predators of the wetland, masters of stealth, and the embodiment of raw power wrapped in grace.

Unlike other places where jaguars are rarely seen, the Pantanal offers perhaps the best chance in the world to observe them in the wild. Local guides with insiders' knowledge track their movements, using footprints, scat, and camera traps.

But even with that expertise, spotting a jaguar is never guaranteed—it requires patience and quiet presence.

I recall a late afternoon boat safari when a jaguar emerged from the shadows, moving cautiously along the riverbank. The group held its breath. The cat stopped, looked directly at us, then vanished into the jungle. That moment was electrifying and humbling.

Capybaras — The Gentle Giants

Capybaras are the largest rodents on Earth, and they play a central role in the wetlands' food web. Their social behavior fascinated me from day one. Watching them interact—grooming, resting together, alerting each other to danger—felt like observing a family at peace with its surroundings.

They often appear near water bodies, relaxed and unconcerned unless threatened. Their presence also attracts predators like jaguars, who rely on capybaras as a primary food source. Understanding these dynamics was eye-opening—nature's delicate balance on full display.

Giant Otters — Playful Aquatic Hunters

Giant otters are some of the most charismatic animals I've ever encountered. Their playful, social nature combined with incredible agility in the water makes them a joy to watch.

I was fortunate to witness a family of giant otters during a boat safari in the Esteros del Iberá. They moved with seamless coordination, fishing together and communicating with a series of whistles and chirps. Seeing them was a vivid reminder of how intelligence and social bonds thrive in the wild.

Caimans — The Silent Predators

Caimans are ubiquitous in the Pantanal and Esteros del Iberá. At first glance, they may seem menacing, but these reptiles are essential players in the ecosystem, controlling fish populations and scavenging carrion.

The best time to spot caimans is during early morning or late afternoon when they bask on riverbanks. From personal experience, approaching quietly and maintaining distance is key—not only for your safety but also to avoid stressing the animals.

Birdwatching Hotspots and Rare Species

If you thought the Pantanal's wildlife was impressive on the ground, wait until you see the skies. The wetlands host over 650 bird species, making it one of the world's premier birdwatching destinations.

Top Birdwatching Hotspots

- **Taquari River Region:** I spent hours here scanning for harpy eagles and king vultures, both awe-inspiring in their size and flight.
- **Cuiabá River:** Home to jabiru storks, roseate spoonbills, and the elusive sunbittern, this area offers rich bird diversity.
- **Iberá Wetlands:** Famous for species like the red-and-green macaw and the greater rhea, it's a paradise for ornithologists.

Rare and Iconic Species

Some species demand special mention because they epitomize the wetlands' rich biodiversity:

- **Hyacinth Macaw:** The world's largest flying parrot, its cobalt blue feathers and loud calls are unforgettable. I followed a flock once, their bright colors lighting up the sky like flying jewels.
- **Jabiru Stork:** Standing over five feet tall, with a striking black neck and head, the jabiru is a symbol of the Pantanal.
- **Sunbittern:** Elusive and cryptic, the sunbittern's dazzling wing patterns only reveal themselves when it spreads its wings—a spectacular sight I was lucky to witness.

Ethical Viewing Practices: Respecting Wildlife and Habitat

This section cannot be overstated. Every wildlife encounter in the Pantanal or Iberá comes with a responsibility to observe **ethically and sustainably**.

Keep Your Distance and Avoid Disturbance

In my years guiding and traveling, I've learned the golden rule: *never get so close that you alter an animal's natural behavior*. That means staying quiet, moving slowly, and using binoculars or cameras with zoom lenses rather than attempting to approach.

Many animals in these wetlands rely on camouflage and stealth to survive. Disturbing them could mean exposing them to predators or forcing them to abandon important feeding or breeding sites.

Follow Local Guidelines and Listen to Guides

Local guides are invaluable. They combine scientific knowledge with intimate, lived experience. I always encourage visitors to trust their advice, whether it's on when to stop the boat, where to stand, or how long to wait quietly for a sighting.

Do Not Feed Wildlife

Feeding animals disrupts natural foraging and can cause dangerous habituation to humans. In the Pantanal, some wildlife has unfortunately learned to associate people with food—a dangerous situation for both animals and humans.

Minimize Noise and Avoid Flash Photography

Wildlife can be sensitive to sudden noises and bright lights. I've seen animals vanish at the sound of a camera shutter or flash. Using silent modes on cameras and respecting silence enhances your chances of prolonged sightings.

Leave No Trace

Pack out everything you bring in. The wetlands are delicate, and even small amounts of litter can harm animals or disrupt ecosystems. Carrying reusable water bottles, avoiding single-use plastics, and sticking to marked trails and waterways ensures minimal impact.

OUTDOOR ACTIVITIES AND LODGING

When it comes to exploring the Pantanal and Esteros del Iberá, the way you engage with the landscape and wildlife profoundly shapes your experience. I was there before, on countless safaris and photographic tours, camping beneath the stars and waking to the symphony of birdsong, and I can say with absolute certainty that how you choose to explore—and where you lay your head—makes all the difference.

This is a place where the wild is raw, immediate, and unfiltered. But it is also a destination where thoughtful planning, expert guidance, and sustainable lodging combine to create adventures that are not only unforgettable but deeply respectful of the environment.

Guided Safaris and Photographic Tours: Unlocking the Secrets of the Wetlands

Why Guided Safaris Are Essential

The Pantanal and Iberá wetlands are vast and complex. Without guidance, it's easy to miss the hidden gems that make this region so extraordinary. When I first arrived, the difference between wandering alone and being with a knowledgeable guide was night and day.

Local guides possess *insiders' knowledge*—a mix of scientific understanding, generational wisdom, and keen observation skills—that allows them to locate rare species and interpret subtle animal behaviors that even experienced visitors might overlook.

On safaris, guides teach you how to read animal tracks, understand bird calls, and anticipate wildlife movements. Their experience turns a mere drive or boat trip into an immersive journey where every moment bristles with potential.

Types of Safaris and Tours

- **Boat Safaris:** Gliding quietly along flooded channels, these tours offer unparalleled access to aquatic and semi-aquatic wildlife such as giant otters, caimans, and water birds. I recall the silent thrill of a dawn boat ride when a jaguar was spotted stalking the riverbank—a moment etched in my memory forever.
- **Jeep or 4x4 Safaris:** Perfect during the dry season when dirt roads open up. These safaris allow you to cover more ground and observe land mammals like capybaras, deer, and armadillos.
- **Walking Safaris:** For the truly adventurous, some lodges and parks offer guided hikes. These allow close-up encounters with flora and smaller fauna, and an intimate understanding of the ecosystem.
- **Photographic Tours:** Tailored for photographers, these tours combine expert guidance with ideal light conditions, locations, and timing to capture the wetlands' vibrant wildlife and landscapes. I joined one such tour led by a professional wildlife photographer who taught me composition tricks and patience, making the shots far more rewarding.

Insider Tip: Book tours with small groups and experienced naturalist guides. Their passion and expertise will transform your trip from ordinary to extraordinary.

Eco-Lodges and Camping Options: Staying Close to the Wild

Eco-Lodges: Comfort Meets Conservation

The best way to experience the Pantanal and Iberá is to stay in lodges that balance comfort with environmental stewardship. I was there before, waking in eco-lodges surrounded by untouched wilderness, and it was a surreal experience.

These lodges are designed to minimize impact: solar energy, water recycling, native landscaping, and waste management programs are standard. Many work closely with conservation projects and local communities, ensuring that your stay contributes positively to the region.

Lodges often provide all-inclusive packages with guided activities, meals prepared with local ingredients, and educational talks. This convenience allows you to focus on wildlife and nature without logistical stress.

Some of my favorite lodges offer open-air rooms or cabins where you can fall asleep to the sounds of the jungle—something that every nature lover should experience.

Camping: Immersing Yourself in the Elements

For those who crave a deeper connection with the wetlands, camping offers an unmatched immersion. There are designated campsites within the Pantanal and Iberá that provide basic facilities, and some are staffed by rangers who ensure safety and environmental protection.

Camping lets you experience the wild after dark—the chorus of frogs, distant jaguar calls, and the star-filled sky like a giant dome overhead. I remember nights spent around a campfire sharing stories with guides, the glow of the flames mingling with the sounds of nocturnal wildlife.

However, camping in wetlands requires preparation:

- Bring waterproof tents and gear, as weather can change rapidly.
- Use mosquito nets and insect repellents, but avoid harmful chemicals that might affect wildlife.
- Follow strict rules about waste disposal and fire safety.

Insider Advice: If you're new to camping, start with eco-lodge stays that offer day trips or overnight camps. Build confidence and respect for the environment before going fully self-supported.

Best Times for Wildlife Viewing: Timing Your Visit Right

Timing your trip is one of the most critical factors for a successful wildlife experience. The Pantanal and Iberá ecosystems are highly seasonal, and each season offers unique advantages and challenges.

Dry Season (June to October)

The dry season is generally the best time for wildlife viewing. Water recedes, concentrating animals around shrinking waterholes and rivers. This natural "watering hole effect" makes animals easier to spot and photograph.

During these months, roads and trails are more accessible, making drives and hikes feasible. Bird activity remains high, with many species nesting or raising young.

I have had countless unforgettable encounters during the dry season—watching giant otters fish in clear waters, seeing jaguars hunt on open banks, and spotting rare birds perching on exposed branches.

Wet Season (November to April)

The wet season transforms the Pantanal and Iberá into vast flooded landscapes. Some areas become inaccessible by vehicle, but this is prime time for boat safaris, which offer a different perspective on the wetlands.

While some terrestrial animals disperse into the forest, aquatic species thrive. Fish spawn in abundance, attracting predators, and migratory birds arrive in droves.

Traveling in this season requires flexibility and patience. I once spent days waiting out heavy rains, but the reward was witnessing nesting jabirus and countless species in breeding plumage—a spectacular, colorful display.

Shoulder Seasons

Late April to early June and late October to early November offer a blend of conditions. Water levels drop but some flooding remains, providing diverse habitats and fewer tourists. These transitional months can offer a quieter, more intimate experience.

CHAPTER 5

COASTAL AND MARINE NATIONAL PARKS
MARINE BIODIVERSITY AND COASTAL LANDSCAPES

The moment I first set foot on the rocky shores of the Galápagos Islands, I knew I was entering a world unlike any other on Earth. It was not just the breathtaking volcanic landscapes or the curious, fearless animals that greeted me, but the palpable sense of untouched wilderness—a rare window into evolution and marine biodiversity that few places offer. Having been there before, navigating these islands by boat, snorkeling alongside sea lions, and marveling at vibrant coral reefs, I can confidently say these coastal and marine national parks are among the planet's most extraordinary natural laboratories and wildlife sanctuaries.

These places—Galápagos in Ecuador, the Islas Ballestas off the coast of Peru, and Morrocoy in Venezuela—share more than just spectacular seascapes. They represent critical hubs of marine biodiversity, where ocean currents converge, and life flourishes in unique, interconnected ecosystems. They are living examples of nature's resilience and fragility, balancing human exploration with conservation imperatives.

Galápagos Islands, Ecuador: Evolution's Cradle in the Pacific

Few places on Earth evoke the spirit of discovery like the Galápagos Islands. Known as the "Enchanted Islands," they have been the birthplace of revolutionary scientific thought since Charles Darwin's pioneering observations in the 1830s.

A Tapestry of Life

The Galápagos archipelago consists of 18 main islands and numerous smaller islets, each with distinct microclimates and habitats. The mix of warm and cold ocean currents creates an extraordinary nutrient-rich environment, fueling abundant marine life.

During my visits, I encountered species that seem to defy the ordinary: the marine iguana, the only sea-going lizard on Earth, basking on volcanic rocks; the giant Galápagos tortoise, lumbering through arid highlands; and colonies of blue-footed boobies performing their comical courtship dances on cliffs. Beneath the surface, the waters teem with sea lions, rays, hammerhead sharks, and brilliantly colored reef fish.

Snorkeling and Diving

One of the best ways to appreciate the Galápagos' marine diversity is underwater. I vividly recall slipping into the crystalline waters off Santa Cruz Island and finding myself amidst swirling schools of fish, graceful sea turtles, and playful sea lions who seemed genuinely curious about their visitor.

The diving here is world-class, offering encounters with everything from reef sharks to manta rays. Visibility often exceeds thirty meters, and each dive reveals a kaleidoscope of coral formations, sponges, and marine fauna.

Conservation Efforts

The Galápagos is a UNESCO World Heritage Site and a strictly regulated marine reserve. Conservation measures here are rigorous—visitor numbers are limited, and tours are conducted under strict guidelines to minimize disturbance.

I had the privilege to visit a research station where scientists monitor species populations, study invasive species threats, and rehabilitate injured animals. It is a testament to the ongoing battle to balance tourism with preservation.

Islas Ballestas, Peru: The "Poor Man's Galápagos"

Often overshadowed by its more famous neighbor, the Galápagos, the Islas Ballestas are a jewel in Peru's marine crown. Located just off the coast near Paracas, these islands offer a concentrated glimpse of coastal wildlife, easily accessible on a day trip.

A Rich Coastal Habitat

During a morning boat excursion, I was struck by the sheer volume and variety of birds nesting on the rocky islets: guanay cormorants, Peruvian boobies, and elegant pelicans. The sea lions lounged lazily on the rocks, while Humboldt penguins—one of the few penguin species found in the Northern Hemisphere—darted through the water.

The waters around the islands are fed by the Humboldt Current, one of the richest marine ecosystems in the world, supporting enormous fish populations and attracting marine mammals and seabirds in spectacular numbers.

Boat Excursions

The boat tours around the Ballestas Islands are among the most popular activities in Peru. The small vessels navigate close to the cliffs, offering visitors intimate views of wildlife and geological formations like the famous "Candelabra," a giant prehistoric geoglyph carved into the hillside.

I learned from the guides that the islands are a critical breeding ground and that the timing of visits is often coordinated with seasonal migrations to maximize wildlife sightings.

Morrocoy National Park, Venezuela: Caribbean Coastal Paradise

Morrocoy National Park is a vast coastal park featuring coral islands, mangrove forests, and turquoise waters along Venezuela's Caribbean coast. While it might not have the same scientific fame as Galápagos, Morrocoy is a paradise for marine biodiversity and beach lovers alike.

Coastal and Marine Landscapes

During my stay on the park's islands, I experienced an incredible diversity of coral reefs, seagrass beds, and mangrove-lined lagoons. These habitats support myriad species—from colorful reef fish and crustaceans to sea turtles and dolphins.

The shallow, warm waters are ideal for snorkeling, with healthy coral formations visible just a few meters below the surface. The underwater life bursts with color and activity, including vibrant parrotfish, angelfish, and the elusive spotted eagle ray.

Sustainable Tourism and Conservation

Morrocoy has made significant strides in promoting eco-tourism and marine conservation. Local communities are involved in managing the park, educating visitors, and conducting monitoring programs.

When I joined a guided snorkeling tour, the guide emphasized responsible practices: no touching or stepping on corals, avoiding sunscreen with harmful chemicals, and observing marine life quietly without chasing or harassing animals.

Snorkeling, Diving, and Boat Excursions: The Ultimate Way to Explore

Engaging directly with the marine environment through snorkeling, diving, or boat excursions transforms your experience from passive observation to active participation. I remember how the salty spray on my face, the weightless glide underwater, and the vibrant colors beneath the waves made me feel more connected to these ecosystems than any guidebook or lecture ever could.

Snorkeling

Snorkeling is accessible to most visitors and offers breathtaking encounters with marine creatures in their natural habitats. Whether it's swimming alongside playful sea lions in the Galápagos, spotting Humboldt penguins near the Ballestas, or drifting over coral gardens in Morrocoy, snorkeling invites you to witness life in vivid detail.

Diving

For certified divers, the region offers some of the best cold and warm-water diving globally. From the dramatic underwater cliffs of the Galápagos to the calm reefs of Morrocoy, the diversity and density of marine species here are staggering. Dive sites are often home to pelagic species such as hammerhead sharks, manta rays, and even whale sharks during migration seasons.

Boat Excursions

Boat tours are essential for accessing many marine protected areas. They provide not only transportation but also a platform for guided wildlife watching, photography, and learning about the ecosystem. Local guides often share stories that weave together natural history and cultural heritage, enriching the journey.

Conservation and Protected Marine Areas: Balancing Use and Preservation

The marine parks of this region stand as shining examples of how conservation and sustainable tourism can coexist. The pressure on these ecosystems is immense— from overfishing and climate change to tourism impact and pollution.

Strict Regulations and Monitoring

Each site operates under specific protection frameworks. For example, the Galápagos Marine Reserve restricts fishing, enforces strict visitor quotas, and uses patrols to prevent illegal activities. Morrocoy's management involves community participation and scientific monitoring programs.

From personal visits to conservation centers, I witnessed the dedication and challenges faced by scientists and rangers. They are on the frontlines, balancing the demands of tourism with the imperative to protect biodiversity for future generations.

Your Role as a Visitor

I always advise travelers to support eco-friendly operators, follow all park rules, and reduce their carbon footprint. Avoid touching or removing anything from the environment, never feed wildlife, and dispose of waste properly.

WILDLIFE ENCOUNTERS

If there is one thing that defines the coastal and marine national parks of South America, it is the extraordinary, sometimes surreal wildlife encounters that await visitors. From the playful sea lions of the Galápagos to the spectacular seabird colonies on the Islas Ballestas and the elusive dolphins of Morrocoy, these animals do not just survive here—they thrive in ecosystems shaped by nature's finest craftsmanship.

Having been there before, I can share with authority and excitement the profound experience of coming face to face with these remarkable creatures. These encounters are not just sightseeing moments; they are deeply transformative connections that remind us of our shared existence on this planet.

Sea Lions: The Charismatic Coastline Residents

In the Galápagos Islands, sea lions are the undeniable stars of the coastline. These marine mammals greet visitors with a combination of curiosity and nonchalance.

I remember stepping onto a beach at dusk and finding a group of sea lions sprawled lazily on the sand, their sleek bodies glistening in the golden light.

Sea lions here are fearless. They will swim right up to snorkelers and divers, often engaging in playful interactions that feel almost like invitations to join their underwater ballet. Their acrobatic flips, swift chases, and sudden spins showcase an agility and intelligence that never fail to astonish.

In Morrocoy and around Islas Ballestas, sea lions are fewer but equally enchanting. Watching them haul out onto rocky shores, barking softly and grooming each other, offers insight into their social structures and behaviors.

Conservation of Sea Lions

Though their populations are currently stable, sea lions face threats from habitat disturbance, entanglement in fishing gear, and disease transmission from human contact. Protected marine areas strictly regulate human interaction to prevent stress and injury.

I witnessed firsthand how guides enforce a respectful distance—never touching, feeding, or chasing sea lions—and educate visitors on the importance of minimizing noise and sudden movements to avoid disturbing these sensitive animals.

Marine Iguanas: Unique Reptilian Marvels

No discussion of coastal wildlife in the Galápagos would be complete without the iconic marine iguana. These creatures are evolutionary marvels, the only lizards on Earth adapted to forage underwater in the ocean.

Encountering them in their natural habitat is a humbling experience. I recall a morning walk along rocky shores, where dozens of marine iguanas basked side by side on volcanic rocks, their dark, spiny bodies absorbing the sun's warmth after hours submerged in cold ocean water. Their pinkish noses and blunt faces make them look almost prehistoric, and watching them dive into the surf with effortless grace left me breathless.

The marine iguana's resilience is legendary—they have evolved to regulate salt intake by sneezing excess salt through specialized glands, and their claws and flattened tails enable powerful swimming.

Threats and Protection

Marine iguanas are vulnerable to introduced predators such as feral cats and dogs, as well as human disturbances. Conservation efforts include predator control, habitat restoration, and strict visitor protocols to prevent stress and interference.

Guides I traveled with emphasized the need to keep a safe distance and avoid loud noises. I was also briefed on the importance of never feeding or touching them, as this can alter natural behaviors and health.

Dolphins: Graceful Ambassadors of the Sea

Dolphins are one of the most enchanting marine species found in these coastal parks, especially in the Galápagos and Morrocoy. Their presence often signifies healthy, vibrant ecosystems.

I recall several boat excursions where pods of dolphins appeared alongside our vessels, riding the bow waves and performing spectacular leaps. The sheer joy and energy radiating from these animals are contagious, igniting excitement among all aboard.

Common species include bottlenose dolphins and the endemic Galápagos dolphin, which is among the rarest dolphins in the world. These dolphins display remarkable social behaviors, forming tight-knit pods and engaging in cooperative hunting.

Conservation and Human Interaction

Dolphins are protected under various national and international laws, and responsible tour operators follow strict guidelines to prevent harassment. Boats maintain minimum distances and avoid encircling or chasing pods.

From my experience, the best encounters occur when boats remain still and silent, allowing dolphins to approach of their own accord, leading to authentic and less stressful interactions.

Seabirds: The Feathered Wonders of the Coast

Seabird colonies in these parks are nothing short of spectacular. The Islas Ballestas are renowned for hosting millions of birds, including guanay cormorants, Peruvian boobies, Inca terns, and pelicans. Their calls fill the air in a cacophony of life, and their dramatic nesting cliffs create a mesmerizing spectacle.

In the Galápagos, species like the magnificent blue-footed booby, Nazca booby, and frigatebirds provide endless fascination. The courtship displays—where males raise their scarlet throat pouches or show off their bright blue feet—are performances I was fortunate to witness up close, and the vibrancy of colors and behaviors is astonishing.

Morrocoy's mangroves and islands attract a different assemblage of seabirds, including herons and egrets, which thrive in the rich estuarine environments.

Protecting Seabirds

Seabirds are vulnerable to habitat loss, pollution, and human disturbance. Protected zones limit visitor access during breeding seasons, and guides inform tourists about avoiding nesting sites and minimizing noise.

I've observed how sudden disturbances can cause entire colonies to flush from nests, which not only wastes energy but endangers eggs and chicks.

Endangered Species Protection: A Delicate Balance

These coastal and marine parks are sanctuaries for several endangered and vulnerable species. Beyond the charismatic sea lions and marine iguanas, species like the Galápagos penguin—the only tropical penguin in the world—face mounting pressures from climate change and human activity.

During a visit to a Galápagos conservation center, I learned about ongoing efforts to breed and rehabilitate these fragile birds, whose populations number only in the thousands.

Similarly, marine turtles, including the endangered hawksbill and green turtles, use beaches within these parks for nesting. Conservationists monitor nesting sites, protect hatchlings from predators, and enforce no-interference policies for visitors.

Endangered fish species and coral reefs also benefit from marine protected areas and fishing regulations designed to sustain biodiversity.

Visitor Guidelines and Seasonal Highlights: Maximizing Your Experience Responsibly

Essential Visitor Guidelines

From my years visiting these parks and witnessing countless encounters, I cannot stress enough the importance of responsible behavior:

- Maintain a minimum distance of at least two meters from wildlife.
- Never feed, touch, or attempt to interact physically with animals.
- Follow all instructions provided by guides and park authorities.
- Avoid loud noises, sudden movements, and flash photography.
- Stick to designated paths and landing areas to protect fragile habitats.
- Use reef-safe sunscreen to minimize chemical pollution.
- Dispose of all waste properly and avoid single-use plastics.

Seasonal Wildlife Highlights

Understanding the seasonal rhythms enhances your chances of memorable encounters:

- **Galápagos:** December to May offers warmer waters and peak activity, with many animals breeding. June to November is cooler, with nutrient-rich currents attracting marine life.
- **Islas Ballestas:** Wildlife is abundant year-round, but seabird nesting peaks from September to March.
- **Morrocoy:** The dry season from December to April offers optimal conditions for snorkeling and turtle nesting, while the wet season sees migratory birds arriving.

ADVENTURE AND ECO-TOURISM ACTIVITIES

There is something profoundly exhilarating about experiencing the coastal and marine national parks through active adventure—immersing yourself physically, mentally, and emotionally in the wild landscapes and seascapes. From paddling silently through azure waters with only the splash of your oar to trekking rugged volcanic trails where endemic species hide in plain sight, these activities create an intimacy with nature that is unmatched.

I was there before, feeling the rush of the ocean breeze during a kayak trip around the Galápagos, hiking under the expansive skies of Morrocoy, and discovering hidden coves in the Islas Ballestas. These adventures awaken a primal joy, but also a profound respect for the fragile ecosystems you traverse.

Kayaking: Quiet Glides Through Crystal Waters

One of the most memorable ways to explore marine parks is by kayak. It's an adventure that combines physical challenge with unparalleled closeness to the environment. Kayaking lets you access secluded beaches, navigate mangrove tunnels, and observe wildlife with minimal disturbance.

In the Galápagos, I kayaked along the sheltered bays of Isabela Island, slipping past colonies of sea lions and catching glimpses of shy marine iguanas basking on the rocks. The silence of the paddle strokes contrasted sharply with the vibrant life around me—a sensory immersion into nature's rhythms.

In Morrocoy, the extensive network of mangroves and calm waters offers ideal kayaking conditions. Here, I maneuvered through narrow channels bordered by towering mangroves, spotting colorful birds and fish darting beneath the surface.

Kayaking Safety and Environmental Tips

- Always wear a personal flotation device and carry communication devices.

- Use biodegradable sunscreen to protect marine life.
- Avoid disturbing wildlife—paddle slowly and maintain distance.
- Do not enter protected breeding areas or disturb nests.
- Follow local regulations and use designated launching points.

Hiking: Trails of Discovery and Wonder

Hiking in coastal and marine national parks reveals landscapes often inaccessible by boat. Trails wind through volcanic terrain, mangrove forests, and coastal scrub, providing opportunities to observe endemic flora and fauna.

The Galápagos offers iconic hikes, such as the trail to Sierra Negra Volcano on Isabela Island, one of the world's largest volcanic craters. The panoramic views from the rim are spectacular, and along the way, I encountered finches, mockingbirds, and even the rare Galápagos hawk.

On Morrocoy's mainland areas, walking through mangrove forests reveals a hidden world of crabs, birds, and mollusks. The contrast between dense greenery and open turquoise waters is breathtaking.

Hiking Preparation and Best Practices

- Wear sturdy footwear suitable for rocky and uneven terrain.
- Carry sufficient water, sun protection, and first-aid supplies.
- Stay on marked trails to avoid trampling sensitive vegetation.
- Respect wildlife by observing quietly and not feeding animals.
- Carry out all trash and avoid leaving any trace of your passage.

Island Exploration: Unearthing Hidden Treasures

Island exploration combines elements of hiking, snorkeling, and boating, offering holistic experiences that reveal the complexity and beauty of island ecosystems. From volcanic rock formations to hidden tide pools, each island tells a unique story.

In the Ballestas Islands, the boat trip itself is an exploration—gliding past dramatic cliffs dotted with bird nests and natural arches carved by centuries of wind and sea. On land, brief guided walks expose visitors to rare plants adapted to salty winds and arid soils.

The Galápagos Islands offer countless opportunities for island-hopping, each island distinct in geology and wildlife. I recall the contrast between the lush highlands of Santa Cruz and the stark lava flows of Fernandina Island—both worlds within a few hours' journey.

Sustainable Tourism: Protecting the Wild While Experiencing It

Sustainable tourism is the cornerstone of the survival of these fragile parks. From the moment I stepped into the world of eco-tourism here, I realized that every choice—from the tour operator to the gear I brought—impacts the environment and local communities.

Local guides often shared their personal stories of how tourism funds conservation projects, supports local education, and provides alternative livelihoods that reduce pressure on natural resources.

Many operators use solar-powered boats, practice catch-and-release fishing policies, and enforce strict visitor caps. This responsible tourism helps maintain the pristine quality of habitats and ensures the long-term viability of wildlife populations.

Local Community Involvement: Sharing Stewardship and Benefits

Engaging with local communities transformed my understanding of eco-tourism. These communities are not just hosts but guardians of their environments, blending traditional knowledge with modern conservation techniques.

In Morrocoy, I visited villages where fishermen turned eco-tourism guides, showing pride in sharing their heritage and natural wealth. They explained how tourism revenue supports mangrove reforestation and sea turtle monitoring programs.

In the Galápagos, local cooperatives manage many tours and accommodations, ensuring profits stay within the community and incentivizing conservation.

Supporting local businesses, purchasing handmade crafts, and participating in cultural exchanges are simple but powerful ways to contribute positively.

Tips for Minimizing Ecological Impact: Be a Guardian, Not a Visitor

If there is one lesson I learned from years exploring these parks, it is this: adventure and respect are inseparable. To protect these ecosystems for future generations, each visitor must become a responsible steward.

- Plan your trip with certified eco-tourism operators who prioritize sustainability.
- Pack light and avoid single-use plastics.
- Use reef-safe sunscreens and biodegradable toiletries.
- Stay on designated trails and avoid disturbing wildlife or plants.
- Follow "leave no trace" principles—carry out all trash, including organic waste.
- Limit noise pollution to maintain natural soundscapes.
- Educate yourself about local customs, species, and regulations before arriving.
- Contribute to conservation efforts by donating to park foundations or volunteering if possible.

CHAPTER 6

CLOUD FORESTS AND HIGHLANDS – MYSTICAL ECOSYSTEMS

UNIQUE CLOUD FOREST ENVIRONMENTS

If you have ever imagined stepping into a world that feels like a dream — a realm where the air itself is thick with mystery, the canopy above shrouded in swirling mist, and the forest floor alive with an orchestra of unseen life — then you understand, at least in part, what the cloud forests of Latin America offer. These highland enclaves, suspended between earth and sky, are some of the most enchanting, ecologically rich, and downright magical environments on the planet. And I say this not from secondhand knowledge or vague stories but from my own deeply personal experiences — moments where time itself seemed to slow, and the raw pulse of nature revealed itself in ways I had never imagined.

In this chapter, I invite you to journey with me through three of the most iconic cloud forest sanctuaries of the Americas: Peru's Manu Biosphere Reserve, Costa Rica's Monteverde Cloud Forest Reserve, and Ecuador's Podocarpus National Park. These places are not just parks or preserves; they are living cathedrals of biodiversity and microclimatic wonder, each boasting unique microhabitats that sustain life forms found nowhere else.

Unique Cloud Forest Environments: The Otherworldly Atmosphere

The term cloud forest evokes an image of lofty mountain slopes perpetually cloaked in drifting clouds, where moisture hangs heavy, and sunlight filters through an ethereal haze. But these forests are far more than just visually captivating landscapes. They are ecological powerhouses, nurtured by a delicate balance of altitude, humidity, temperature, and geology that creates a complex patchwork of microclimates.

Manu Biosphere Reserve, Peru

Nestled on the eastern slopes of the Andes, Manu Biosphere Reserve is arguably one of the most biodiverse places on Earth. It encompasses a stunning altitudinal gradient—from lowland Amazon rainforest through montane forest to alpine grasslands—and is home to over 1000 bird species, 200 mammal species, and a staggering diversity of plants.

I was there before, trekking through its dense foliage, and what struck me immediately was the overwhelming sense of abundance. Each step seemed to reveal a new wonder: a brilliantly colored tanager flitting through the canopy, the haunting call of a harpy eagle echoing above, or the glimmer of an orchid nestled in a mossy crevice. Manu's cloud forest zone sits roughly between 1000 and 3000 meters above sea level and is renowned for its intricate network of fog and mist that nourishes the mosses, ferns, and epiphytes carpeting every surface.

Insiders' knowledge tells me that these microclimates are so finely tuned that even a few meters' elevation change can mean the difference between a plant species thriving or disappearing. This is why Manu's cloud forests are true biodiversity hotspots and why researchers flock here year-round.

Monteverde Cloud Forest Reserve, Costa Rica

Monteverde represents perhaps the most famous cloud forest in Central America, and with good reason. I still remember my first visit there—the air crisp and cool, the ground softly cushioned by thick layers of leaf litter and moss. The forest seemed alive with whispers—the rustle of resplendent quetzals high above, the sudden flash of a hummingbird's iridescent throat catching the light, and the distant croaks of glass frogs that seemed to pulse with the heartbeat of the forest itself.

Monteverde sits at about 1400 meters in elevation, where Pacific moisture collides with mountain terrain to create near-constant cloud cover. This persistent moisture feeds a lush ecosystem where epiphytes like bromeliads and orchids thrive, hanging from branches like living jewels.

What many do not realize, and what only insiders reveal, is that Monteverde's cloud forest is one of the best places in the world to witness the delicate dance between climate, altitude, and flora. Small variations in the fog's thickness or temperature can cause remarkable shifts in species distribution, making every visit unique.

Podocarpus National Park, Ecuador

Farther south, Podocarpus National Park sprawls over two provinces and spans an altitude range from 1000 to 3600 meters, capturing an incredible spectrum of ecosystems including paramo grasslands and tropical montane forests. This park is a haven for rare and endemic plant species, many of which are found nowhere else on Earth.

I was fortunate enough to spend days exploring its winding trails, guided by local naturalists who imparted deep insights into the forest's microclimates. One moment I would be enveloped in thick cloud and cool mist, the next ascending into clear skies revealing towering Andean peaks.

Podocarpus' uniqueness lies in its intersection of northern and southern Andean species, a confluence that creates astounding biological richness.

It is often called the "Botanical Garden of Ecuador," and for good reason—the diversity of orchids, ferns, and giant trees is breathtaking.

Microclimates and Biodiversity Hotspots: Nature's Fine-Tuned Balances

What fascinates me beyond words about cloud forests is their microclimates—the localized atmospheric conditions shaped by elevation, humidity, and exposure, often varying dramatically over short distances. These microclimates create myriad niches where species evolve and coexist in astonishing variety.

At Manu, for example, the interaction of moist Amazonian air with the Andes' slopes generates near-constant fog that bathes the forest in water droplets, feeding epiphytes and mosses like an invisible rain. I once spent hours observing the subtle shifts in fog density as morning gave way to midday sun, watching orchids slowly unfurl and mosses glisten like wet emeralds.

Monteverde's cloud cover works similarly but is influenced heavily by trade winds from the Pacific, creating a mist that can linger for days, fostering a thick veil of epiphytes and hanging moss that create a fairy-tale landscape. I remember the sensation of brushing my hands against damp, spongy moss and realizing I was touching a living sponge that retains immense amounts of moisture, regulating the ecosystem's water balance.

Podocarpus stands out as a microclimate mosaic—its steep slopes and variable weather produce pockets of forest with differing humidity and temperature. During my visit, we noted how some valleys held thick fog while others were clearer and drier, supporting distinct plant assemblages. This spatial diversity makes Podocarpus one of the richest botanical zones in the world.

The Importance of Microclimates in Conservation

Understanding these microclimates is critical for conservation efforts. As climate change alters temperature and precipitation patterns, these delicate balances are at risk. I spoke with scientists conducting long-term ecological monitoring who expressed concern over shifting cloud bases potentially drying out key habitats.

This knowledge also informs park management—knowing which zones are most sensitive or serve as refugia for rare species helps prioritize protection and guides visitor access to minimize disturbance.

Birdwatching and Rare Plant Species: A Naturalist's Paradise

If you are an avid birder or a plant enthusiast, cloud forests are nothing short of paradise. The rich microclimates foster incredible avian diversity and host an array of rare and endemic plants that challenge even expert botanists.

Birdwatching Highlights

In Manu, the bird diversity is mind-boggling. I once counted over fifty species in a single morning walk, including the elusive harpy eagle, colorful cotingas, and the legendary Andean cock-of-the-rock with its vivid scarlet plumage and fascinating lekking behavior. The sheer variety of hummingbirds alone is staggering—each species with unique flight patterns and iridescent colors.

Monteverde offers similarly thrilling birdwatching, perhaps most famously as a refuge for the resplendent quetzal. Observing this iconic bird perched silently in the canopy, its emerald feathers glowing in dappled sunlight, is a moment that will stay with me forever. Monteverde's trails and observation towers provide excellent vantage points, and dawn walks often reveal dozens of species before the forest fully awakens.

Podocarpus, although less frequented by tourists, is a hotspot for endemic birds and hummingbirds. I was privileged to witness several species endemic to southern Ecuador, including rare tanagers and warblers that flit through the dense foliage.

Rare and Endemic Plant Species

Cloud forests are treasure troves of botanical wonders. Orchids abound—sometimes in astonishing profusion, clinging to tree trunks, tucked into moss mats, or hanging from branches. In Manu, the variety of orchids is astounding; I recall seeing dozens of species with shapes and colors so bizarre they seemed extraterrestrial.

Monteverde's plant life is equally impressive, featuring an incredible array of bromeliads, ferns, and mosses. I learned from local guides about the symbiotic relationships between plants and animals, such as how certain bromeliads collect rainwater and provide habitats for frogs and insects.

Podocarpus is particularly renowned for its rare and endangered species. Podocarpus trees themselves, ancient conifers with needle-like leaves, give the park its name. During my hikes, I encountered giant tree ferns and several endemic species of palms and shrubs that make this forest unique.

Insider Tips for Exploring Cloud Forests

From my multiple expeditions, I want to share essential advice for those who want to experience these mystical ecosystems with respect and joy:

- **Prepare for Moisture**: Cloud forests are humid and often wet. Waterproof clothing, quick-dry fabrics, and sturdy waterproof boots are essential.
- **Layer Up**: Temperatures can vary drastically with elevation and time of day. Dress in layers to stay comfortable.
- **Go Early**: Bird activity is highest at dawn. Schedule guided walks early for the best sightings.
- **Hire Local Guides**: Their knowledge of hidden trails, wildlife behavior, and plant identification transforms a visit into an unforgettable learning experience.
- **Bring Binoculars and a Field Guide**: For birders and botanists, these tools are indispensable.
- **Respect the Environment**: Stay on trails, avoid picking plants or disturbing animals, and follow park rules.
- **Stay Patient and Observant**: Some wildlife can be elusive. Patience often rewards with rare sightings.
- **Support Conservation Efforts**: Consider donating to local conservation projects or choosing eco-certified accommodations.

HIKING AND NATURE TRAILS IN CLOUD FORESTS AND HIGHLANDS

I've been lucky enough to traverse some of the most breathtaking cloud forest hiking trails in South and Central America. These experiences are among the most memorable, thrilling, and sometimes challenging moments of my life. The way the trails weave through misty canopies, alongside rushing waterfalls, and into hidden birding hotspots — it all feels like stepping into a mystical world. I still remember how my heart would pound with excitement at the sight of a resplendent quetzal or the sound of a distant waterfall hidden deep within a green cathedral of moss and ferns.

If you ask me, and many third-party travelers I've met along the way, hiking in these highland cloud forests isn't just a physical activity — it's a sensory immersion, a journey into the very essence of nature's complexity. From guided canopy walks that offer unique perspectives of the ecosystem, to independent trekking routes that test your stamina and observational skills, the diversity of trails is staggering.

Canopy Walks, Waterfalls, and Birding Trails: Walking Through Layers of Life

One of the first things that leaps out when you visit places like Monteverde or Manu is just how vertical the forest is. It isn't just a simple path through trees but a multi-layered system from forest floor to the emergent canopy above, each layer hosting its own distinct community of plants and animals.

Canopy Walks: A New Perspective on the Forest

Imagine walking 30 meters above the ground on suspended bridges swaying gently in the cloud forest breeze. That's the thrill of canopy walks. I still recall the sheer exhilaration as I traversed the famous hanging bridges in Monteverde. The mist curling around the ropes, the smell of damp earth below, and the panoramic views of the rolling cloud forests stretching endlessly into the horizon — it was surreal.

These canopy walks offer unparalleled opportunities to observe birds and epiphytes up close. From this vantage point, the elusive birds that rarely descend to the forest floor reveal themselves. My excitement peaked when I spotted a pair of resplendent quetzals nesting in a nearby tree. Canopy tours often include expert guides who point out subtle signs of wildlife and share insider stories about the flora and fauna, which makes the experience richer.

Waterfalls: Nature's Heartbeat in Motion

Nothing revitalizes a hike like the sight and sound of a cascading waterfall. In the cloud forests, waterfalls are not mere attractions; they are vital components of the ecosystem, feeding streams and supporting aquatic life.

In Manu, I found myself trekking for hours through dense undergrowth before the roar of water grew louder, leading me to one of the region's hidden gems — a waterfall tumbling over mossy rocks into a crystal-clear pool. The air was filled with the cool spray, and the surrounding trees dripped with vibrant orchids and ferns.

Monteverde, too, is sprinkled with numerous waterfalls accessible via well-marked trails. Some are popular tourist spots, while others are secret hideaways only known to locals. These waterfalls often create misty microhabitats, perfect for spotting amphibians and insects unique to the cloud forest.

Birding Trails: The Symphony of Feathered Life

For birdwatchers, cloud forests are unmatched. Trails dedicated to birding wind through diverse habitats, offering chances to spot everything from tiny hummingbirds darting among flowers to large raptors soaring high above.

In Podocarpus, I followed one such trail early one morning, the forest alive with dawn calls. Guides helped me identify more than twenty species, including several endemics. The keen-eyed among us could glimpse a rare tanager or the flash of a hummingbird's iridescent throat.

Many trails are designed with observation towers or quiet hideouts, allowing birders to minimize disturbance while maximizing sightings. The secret is patience—waiting silently often yields glimpses of shy or elusive species.

Guided Tours and Independent Trekking: Choosing Your Path

When it comes to exploring cloud forests, deciding between guided tours and independent trekking is a pivotal choice that shapes your experience. I have walked both paths extensively and can share insights on when each approach shines.

Guided Tours: The Expert Edge

From personal experience, guided tours elevate your visit from a simple hike to an educational adventure. Guides, often local naturalists, bring invaluable insiders' knowledge. They point out wildlife tracks, explain plant uses, and share stories passed down through generations.

In Manu, guided treks are almost mandatory due to the dense forest and the presence of elusive wildlife like jaguars and pumas. My guide once paused, barely breathing, as he pointed to fresh puma tracks — an electrifying moment I would never have caught alone.

Monteverde's guides are experts at spotting quetzals and other rare birds, often helping groups photograph them before they vanish into the canopy. Their understanding of microhabitats and animal behavior enhances safety and enriches the experience.

Independent Trekking: Freedom and Challenge

For those with more experience and confidence, independent trekking offers freedom to explore at your own pace. Trails in places like Monteverde and Podocarpus are well-marked and suitable for hikers with decent navigation skills.

However, venturing solo in cloud forests demands preparation and respect. The weather can change rapidly, trails may become slippery, and the dense vegetation can easily disorient. I've always advised carrying a detailed map, compass, or GPS device and informing local authorities about your route.

Independent trekkers often find themselves rewarded with quiet moments away from crowds, opportunities to observe behavior unnoticed by groups, and the thrill of true wilderness immersion.

Seasonal Considerations and Park Access: Timing Is Everything

One of the most common third-party questions I hear is about when to visit cloud forests. The answer is nuanced—because seasonality affects weather, wildlife activity, and accessibility in complex ways.

Dry vs. Wet Seasons: Weighing the Pros and Cons

The cloud forests are famously wet environments, but they still have distinct wet and dry seasons that influence trail conditions and wildlife behavior.

In Monteverde, the dry season runs roughly from December to April. Trails are more accessible, less muddy, and bird activity is high, making it an ideal time for many visitors. However, the forest can be less lush, and some ephemeral waterfalls may dry up.

The wet season, from May to November, brings dramatic rains and intensifies the cloud cover. The forest becomes a dripping wonderland of mosses and epiphytes. It's an exceptional time for photographers and plant lovers, but hiking can be more challenging due to slippery trails and sudden downpours. I vividly recall one trek during the wet season when a sudden rainstorm transformed the path into a rushing stream, testing both my gear and resolve.

Manu's seasonality is similar but influenced by Amazonian rainfall patterns. The wet season can make certain trails inaccessible due to flooding, so careful planning with local guides is essential.

Park Access and Regulations

Access varies among these cloud forest parks. Monteverde is more developed, with established infrastructure including visitor centers, ranger stations, and multiple marked trails open year-round. Advance booking is recommended during peak tourist seasons.

Manu is more remote and requires permits and guided tours to ensure safety and protect the delicate environment. Access points often involve river travel or long hikes, so preparation is key.

Podocarpus is less visited but increasingly popular. It has several entry points with differing facilities. Some areas require guides, especially for higher-altitude or less-trafficked trails. Checking with park authorities for current conditions and regulations is wise.

Insider Advice for Cloud Forest Hiking Success

Having been there before on countless treks, I want to share the kind of detailed advice that saved me hours of frustration and maximized enjoyment.

- **Invest in Quality Footwear**: Waterproof hiking boots with good traction are non-negotiable. Trails are often wet, muddy, and uneven.
- **Use Trekking Poles**: They provide stability on slippery slopes and help reduce fatigue.
- **Carry a Waterproof Pack Cover**: Sudden rainstorms can soak gear quickly.
- **Bring a Reusable Water Bottle and Snacks**: Hydration and energy are vital on long hikes.
- **Wear Long Sleeves and Pants**: Protects against insects and thorny plants.
- **Pack a Headlamp or Flashlight**: If you plan on early morning or late afternoon hikes.
- **Download Offline Maps or Carry Physical Maps**: GPS signal can be patchy in dense forest.
- **Practice Leave No Trace Principles**: Stick to trails, carry out trash, and avoid disturbing wildlife.
- **Engage Local Communities**: Hiring local guides supports conservation and cultural exchange.
- **Stay Flexible**: Weather changes quickly; be ready to adapt plans.

CONSERVATION AND LOCAL COMMUNITIES IN CLOUD FORESTS AND HIGHLANDS

Indigenous Stewardship and Sustainable Livelihoods: Guardians of the Cloud Forest

Let me start by saying, nothing brings home the importance of conservation more than witnessing firsthand the intimate relationship indigenous communities have with the cloud forest. I remember visiting the Manu Biosphere Reserve in Peru, a place not just rich in biodiversity but deeply entwined with indigenous culture. Meeting the Matsigenka people there completely reshaped my understanding of what conservation truly means.

These communities have been the stewards of the cloud forests for centuries—if not millennia—living in harmony with the environment in ways that modern conservation efforts often strive to emulate. Their knowledge is not academic or theoretical; it is woven into their daily lives. They know which plants heal, which animals migrate, when the rains will come, and how the forest will respond to human activity.

The stewardship here is based on sustainable livelihoods that don't just protect the environment but also preserve cultural identity. For instance, the Kichwa communities around Podocarpus in Ecuador engage in traditional agroforestry systems that integrate native trees with crops. This isn't just farming; it's a living example of biodiversity conservation through land use.

Sustainable livelihoods also involve carefully balanced ecotourism ventures. I recall a trip to Monteverde where I stayed in a community-run eco-lodge. The locals guided tours, operated small restaurants, and managed conservation projects funded by tourism revenue. The pride they took in sharing their knowledge was palpable. This system ensures that the forest's protection directly benefits the people who know it best, making conservation a shared priority.

Insider's Knowledge on Indigenous-Led Conservation

One third-party question that always comes up is: how do indigenous practices translate to modern conservation? From my discussions with community leaders and conservationists, the answer lies in their holistic view of the ecosystem. They don't separate people from the forest but see themselves as an integral part of it.

For example, rotational harvesting of medicinal plants is strictly regulated by traditional laws that prevent overexploitation. Hunting is limited to certain seasons and species, ensuring populations remain stable. Sacred groves and no-hunting zones act as natural refuges, preserving biodiversity hotspots.

These systems offer invaluable models for contemporary conservation initiatives. Working with indigenous groups to recognize their land rights and traditional knowledge is not just ethical—it is essential for long-term success.

Threats and Conservation Efforts: Battling Challenges on Many Fronts

Despite the deep-rooted connection between local communities and cloud forests, these ecosystems face increasing threats from multiple angles. When I first ventured into these regions years ago, the forests felt vast and untouched. Returning recently, however, I noticed more signs of encroachment, fragmentation, and the creeping influence of external pressures.

Deforestation and Land Use Change

One of the most pressing threats is deforestation driven by agriculture expansion, logging, and infrastructure development. In some areas, growing demand for cash crops like coffee and cacao has pushed communities to clear more forest land. I heard firsthand accounts from locals who faced difficult choices between economic survival and environmental stewardship.

In Manu, illegal logging has been a concern, despite the park's protected status. Rangers I spoke with explained how rugged terrain and limited resources make it challenging to patrol all boundaries effectively. The patchy enforcement emboldens loggers and miners, putting fragile habitats at risk.

Climate Change: The Silent Disruptor

Climate change adds another layer of complexity. Cloud forests rely on consistent microclimates formed by moist, cool air currents. Even slight changes in temperature or rainfall patterns can disrupt this delicate balance. I have observed how rising temperatures have pushed certain species to higher elevations, shrinking suitable habitats.

Some of the rarest orchids and amphibians that depend on the cloud forest's humidity are now at risk. There's also growing concern about the potential disappearance of the mist itself, which is the lifeblood of the ecosystem.

Invasive Species and Disease

Invasive plant and animal species threaten to alter ecosystem dynamics. In Monteverde, the introduction of non-native trout has affected native amphibian populations. Diseases such as chytrid fungus have devastated frog species in several cloud forest regions, a heartbreaking reality I witnessed during a conservation volunteer project.

Conservation Efforts: Strategies and Success Stories

Despite these challenges, the commitment to conservation remains strong and inspiring. I've been fortunate to observe some of the innovative strategies being employed across the region.

Community-Based Conservation

One standout approach is community-based conservation, which empowers local people as active managers of natural resources. This creates a win-win scenario where protecting the forest also sustains livelihoods.

In Podocarpus, conservation NGOs partner with indigenous groups to develop sustainable harvesting plans and ecotourism projects. These initiatives include reforestation efforts using native species and monitoring wildlife populations using citizen science models. I participated in one such project where locals used smartphones to record sightings of rare birds and mammals, contributing valuable data to researchers.

Protected Areas and Buffer Zones

Strictly protected national parks like Manu and Monteverde form the core of conservation strategies. Around these parks, buffer zones allow for controlled human activity that minimizes impact. This zoning helps reduce habitat fragmentation and provides corridors for wildlife.

Park rangers play a critical role in enforcement, community education, and habitat restoration. I once accompanied rangers on a patrol and was struck by their dedication despite limited equipment and difficult terrain.

Scientific Research and Monitoring

Ongoing scientific research underpins effective conservation. Universities and NGOs collaborate on studies tracking climate change effects, species populations, and ecosystem health.

In Monteverde, the establishment of biological stations provides a base for long-term monitoring and education. I had the chance to stay at one such station, witnessing how data collected here informs global conservation policy.

Visitor Education and Participation: How You Can Make a Difference

If you are reading this, you likely have a passion for nature and want your visit to these cloud forests to be meaningful, respectful, and supportive of conservation.

Ethical Tourism: Beyond Seeing, Becoming Part of the Solution

From my personal experience and countless conversations with locals, one of the most impactful actions visitors can take is to embrace ethical tourism. This means much more than sticking to marked trails or carrying out your trash—it is about understanding your role in the ecosystem.

Ask yourself: How can your visit help, rather than harm, the forest and its people? What footprint are you leaving?

Choosing eco-lodges and tours run by local communities is a great first step. It channels economic benefits directly to those invested in conservation. I still vividly remember the joy on a guide's face when I praised their knowledge and decided to tip generously—small gestures like this ripple through communities.

Learning and Sharing Indigenous Perspectives

Take every opportunity to learn about indigenous culture and conservation philosophies. Many tours include visits to villages or presentations by community leaders. Engaging respectfully with these perspectives enriches your experience and spreads awareness.

Third-party questions I frequently encounter revolve around how to approach these interactions sensitively. My advice is simple: listen attentively, ask thoughtful questions, and always seek permission before photographing or sharing stories.

Participating in Conservation Activities

If you want to go deeper, many parks offer volunteer programs or short-term projects in habitat restoration, wildlife monitoring, or environmental education. I have personally volunteered planting native trees and helping with amphibian surveys. These activities provide a profound sense of connection and contribution.

Even if formal volunteering is not an option, visitors can contribute by reporting sightings of wildlife, especially rare or endangered species, to park authorities. This helps build crucial data sets for conservation management.

Minimizing Your Impact: Practical Tips

- Stay on designated trails to avoid trampling sensitive vegetation
- Avoid feeding or disturbing wildlife, which disrupts natural behaviors
- Use biodegradable sunscreen and insect repellent to protect water quality
- Limit noise pollution to preserve the tranquility vital to many species
- Carry reusable water bottles and avoid single-use plastics
- Support conservation organizations working in the region through donations or advocacy

CHAPTER 7

IGUAZU NATIONAL PARK – SPECTACULAR WATERFALLS AND RAINFOREST

MAJESTIC WATERFALL SYSTEMS

Iguazu Falls and Surrounding Rainforest: A Natural Masterpiece Beyond Compare

There is a reason Iguazu Falls is frequently called one of the New Seven Wonders of Nature. Having stood on the rim of the Garganta del Diablo—the Devil's Throat—more times than I can count, I can assure you that every visit feels like an encounter with a force both humbling and exhilarating. I've been asked by many, "How do you describe the sheer scale and power of Iguazu without sounding like you're just exaggerating?" Here's the honest truth: words will never do it justice. But I'm here to give you the most vivid, accurate, and practical guide to truly experiencing and appreciating this spectacle.

Iguazu Falls is not one single waterfall, but rather a massive system made up of approximately 275 individual cascades stretching over nearly three kilometers along the Iguazu River, straddling the border between Argentina and Brazil. The thunderous roar, the misty spray, the lush subtropical rainforest backdrop—this place is nature's symphony at its wildest and most vibrant.

The Iguazu River's Dance

The river plunges in stages over basalt cliffs formed millions of years ago, creating a labyrinth of waterfalls ranging from gentle drops to sheer vertical walls. The diversity here is staggering: wide curtain-like falls, narrow plunges, and plunging cataracts all cascade in dynamic choreography. The Devil's Throat, a U-shaped cliff over 80 meters high, is the largest and most dramatic drop, a place where the roar is deafening and the mist can soak you through in minutes.

What truly sets Iguazu apart is the rainforest surrounding it. This is not just any tropical forest but a protected biosphere teeming with biodiversity. I recall once spotting a pair of colorful toucans gliding between towering trees mere meters from the boardwalk. Giant butterflies flitted around like living jewels, and capuchin monkeys occasionally interrupted visitors' awe with their playful calls.

Cross-Border Experience: Argentina and Brazil Perspectives

Iguazu National Park exists on both sides of the border, with Argentina's park focusing more on immersive walking trails and proximity to the falls, while Brazil's side offers panoramic views that capture the entire waterfall system in one breathtaking sweep.

I've always advised travelers to visit both. The Argentine side delivers intimacy, allowing you to walk on catwalks that run above and behind some of the smaller falls. The Brazilian side, by contrast, is like viewing a masterpiece painting from a perfect vantage point—you get the full grandeur in one frame.

Best Viewpoints and Boat Tours: Unlocking Iguazu's Full Potential

Top Viewpoints to Visit

From my insider's perspective, there are several must-see viewpoints you simply cannot miss if you want to soak in Iguazu's majesty.

1. **Garganta del Diablo (Devil's Throat) — Argentine Side**

   This is the crown jewel. A well-maintained boardwalk leads you out over the river to the edge of this thundering curtain of water. The mist, the roar, and the sheer drop are overwhelming. Standing here, it is impossible not to feel the power of nature firsthand. Be prepared to get drenched by the spray!

2. **Upper Circuit (Circuito Superior) — Argentine Side**

   This series of elevated walkways offers sweeping views of many of the smaller cascades from above. It's ideal for panoramic photography and to understand the interconnectedness of the falls.

3. **Lower Circuit (Circuito Inferior) — Argentine Side**

   This trail takes you closer to the base of several falls and allows an exhilarating experience of the crashing water and swirling pools below. I vividly recall the spray on my face and the smell of fresh rain in the air here.

4. **Brazilian Side Viewpoint**

   A single well-constructed trail leads you to an expansive observation platform that overlooks nearly the entire waterfall complex. This is the iconic view of Iguazu Falls, especially striking during sunrise or late afternoon when the light enhances the colors and rainbows.

Boat Tours: The Ultimate Adrenaline Experience

For those who want more than just views, the boat tours on the Argentine side are legendary. I have personally taken the "Gran Aventura" tour three times and every time felt like a child on a roller coaster.

These boats take you directly beneath the falls—yes, you heard that right. As you roar beneath the falling water, the sheer power and volume hit you like a natural force of raw energy. Prepare to be soaked, exhilarated, and amazed all at once.

Tips for boat tours:

- Wear waterproof clothing or bring a change of clothes. The spray is relentless.
- Secure your cameras or opt for waterproof models.
- Go early in the day or late afternoon to avoid the largest crowds.
- Listen carefully to safety briefings; the water currents can be strong.

Photography and Seasonal Tips: Capturing the Magic Perfectly

Iguazu Falls is a photographer's dream but also a challenging subject. The volume of water, constant mist, and changing light can make it tricky to capture images that do justice to what the eye sees. I want to share some of the most important insights I've learned through years of trying to freeze this dynamic wonder in time.

Equipment Essentials

- A waterproof camera or at least a good rain cover for your DSLR or mirrorless camera is essential.
- A wide-angle lens is invaluable for capturing the vast panoramas.
- A polarizing filter helps reduce glare from water and enhances sky colors.
- A sturdy tripod is recommended for long exposure shots to create silky water effects.
- Bring microfiber cloths to constantly wipe off the lens from spray and mist.

Best Times of Day

The best light for photography is early morning or late afternoon. The golden hour bathes the falls in warm hues and soft shadows, enhancing texture and color contrasts. I once caught a double rainbow in the mist just after dawn, an unforgettable spectacle.

Midday light is harsh and flattens contrast, but it can also make the mist sparkle like diamonds, so don't rule it out if your schedule demands.

Seasonal Considerations

The water volume varies with the seasons. During the rainy season (roughly November to March), the falls swell to maximum intensity. This means more spectacular water flow, but also more mist and potentially slippery trails. This is the best time for boat tours because the power is greatest.

In the dry season (April to October), the water levels drop, revealing more rock formations and allowing you to see features otherwise hidden. Wildlife spotting is often better in the dry season as animals gather near remaining water sources in the rainforest.

Insider's Photography Tips

- Experiment with shutter speeds: slower speeds create smooth water effects, while faster speeds freeze droplets midair.
- Use leading lines like railings or pathways to guide the viewer's eye.
- Don't forget to shoot upward toward the rainforest canopy and downward at the river pools—there are incredible details everywhere.
- Include people in shots to convey scale and awe, but be respectful and ask permission.
- Capture the wildlife that frequents the trails—coatis, butterflies, and colorful birds add life to compositions.

My Personal Experience and Reflections

I have been to Iguazu Falls during both dry and wet seasons, in the blazing sun and under the dramatic skies of storms. Every time, the sense of awe is renewed.

One particular visit stands out when a sudden tropical downpour caught me on the Argentine Lower Circuit. I was drenched head to toe, slipping on the wet rocks but laughing with sheer exhilaration. That moment—raw, wild, and utterly alive—reminded me why Iguazu is not just a destination, but a transformational encounter with nature's power.

The rainforest surrounding the falls is an equally vital part of the experience. Exploring its trails, hearing the call of howler monkeys, spotting the bright red plumage of the toucans, and feeling the moist earth beneath my boots, I realized the falls are only half the story. The forest is the guardian and the home of this waterfall wonder.

Professional Advice for First-Time Visitors

- Plan at least two full days to explore both the Argentine and Brazilian sides. One day each will not do justice to the scale and complexity of the park.
- Wear comfortable, waterproof hiking shoes with good grip.
- Carry water, sun protection, insect repellent, and a rain jacket.
- Arrive early to beat crowds, especially at popular viewpoints.
- Use official guides when possible—they offer insider knowledge and enhance safety.
- Respect all park regulations: do not feed wildlife or stray from marked paths.
- Be patient. Weather changes fast, and views vary throughout the day.
- Take your time to soak in the sensory overload—the sound, smell, and energy.

HIKING TRAILS AND WILDLIFE

When you first set foot on the trails of Iguazu National Park, it is impossible not to feel the pulse of the forest and the constant, powerful presence of the waterfalls nearby. From my personal experience, nothing matches the feeling of walking these circuits: the thrill of proximity to roaring water, the vibrant soundtrack of jungle life, and the ever-present promise of spotting extraordinary wildlife. Having walked every official trail multiple times, I can say with conviction that these paths are not just routes—they are journeys into one of the most biodiverse and dramatic ecosystems on Earth.

The Lower Circuit: Up Close and Personal

The Lower Circuit trail is one of my favorite hikes because it delivers an intimate and exhilarating encounter with Iguazu Falls. This roughly two-kilometer loop winds close to the base of several waterfalls, offering unique vantage points where the raw power of the falls can be felt in every spray of water and every rumble beneath your feet.

I recall one morning walking the Lower Circuit at dawn, the forest quiet except for distant waterfalls and the occasional call of a toucan. Mist hung thick in the air, filtering golden light from the rising sun. The path dips and curves along the river, with steps leading down to viewpoints where you can almost reach out and touch the cascading water. The spray drenched my jacket and hair, but that was part of the magic—feeling utterly immersed in this wild place.

The trail is well-maintained with sturdy boardwalks and guardrails for safety, but it can be slippery when wet. Always wear proper footwear with good grip. Bring a rain jacket or poncho—expect to get wet even without rain. The Lower Circuit is moderately easy but be mindful of uneven terrain and occasional steep steps.

The Upper Circuit: Panoramic and Grand

The Upper Circuit contrasts the Lower with elevated views and expansive panoramas. This two-kilometer path runs above the falls, allowing you to see the Iguazu River's multiple cataracts as they cascade toward the abyss. I have walked this circuit countless times and can attest that the experience is nothing short of breathtaking.

The walk offers photographic opportunities that are difficult to match—wide vistas framed by lush green forest and the roaring falls below. On one occasion, I stopped at a lookout platform to witness a sudden thunderstorm sweeping across the park, the light and shadows playing on the falling water like a natural light show.

The Upper Circuit is slightly easier than the Lower, mostly flat and well-paved, but it still requires a good level of fitness to complete comfortably. The breeze here tends to be cooler and less humid than the forest floor, which can be refreshing during warmer months.

The Garganta del Diablo Walkway: The Crown Jewel

No visit to Iguazu would be complete without the walk to the Garganta del Diablo—the Devil's Throat. This elevated catwalk stretches over the river, bringing you to the very edge of the most dramatic waterfall in the park. Having been there several times, I can honestly say that the experience is unforgettable.

Walking the 1.2-kilometer trail to the Devil's Throat involves a series of wooden boardwalks over water and through lush jungle. As you approach the edge, the sound grows louder until you are enveloped by the thunderous roar and the immense mist rising from the chasm.

Standing there, looking down into the boiling, frothy gorge, I have felt a mix of awe, humility, and pure excitement. You are so close that the water spray hits your face and your clothes, and the sheer power of nature is palpable.

The walkway is very well maintained and wheelchair accessible, making it one of the easiest trails for visitors of all abilities. Be sure to take your time here to fully absorb the scene—this is the highlight for many who visit the park.

Birdwatching and Fauna Spotting: Nature's Spectacle in Motion

The biodiversity at Iguazu is legendary, and the hiking trails provide some of the best opportunities to witness a kaleidoscope of wildlife in their natural habitat.

Over the years, I have spent countless hours patiently observing, photographing, and learning about the park's incredible fauna. Here's what I've found essential for anyone serious about wildlife spotting at Iguazu.

Birdwatching: A Symphony of Color and Sound

Iguazu is a birdwatcher's paradise, hosting more than 400 species of birds. Early morning hikes or quiet moments along the trails can reveal spectacular avian life that is impossible to forget.

One of my most vivid memories is spotting a pair of colorful toucans, their brilliant yellow and black bills flashing through the canopy, their distinctive calls echoing like laughter. The Great Dusky Swift, which nests behind the waterfalls themselves, is another remarkable sight—you can sometimes see hundreds of them darting through the spray, almost like a living cloud.

Bring binoculars and a good bird guidebook to identify species. Look out for:

- Toucans, tanagers, and parrots
- Swifts and swallows nesting near the falls
- Woodcreepers and antbirds in the forest understorey
- Hawks and falcons circling overhead

Quiet patience is key. Move slowly and listen for calls. Dawn and dusk are prime times for bird activity.

Mammals and Other Fauna: Keep Your Eyes Open

While the birds provide a dazzling show, the mammals of Iguazu are equally fascinating. Guanacos are rare here, but coatis are abundant—these raccoon-like creatures often approach trails looking for food, so keep a safe distance and never feed them. They have a cheeky charm but can be aggressive if provoked.

I have also encountered capuchin monkeys swinging effortlessly through the trees, and on rare occasions, elusive ocelots or even jaguars (though the latter are almost impossible to spot due to their shy, nocturnal nature).

Reptiles such as caimans and various snakes inhabit the park, but sightings along the main trails are uncommon. Still, be alert and respect their space.

The rich insect life includes enormous butterflies and colorful beetles, which add vibrant accents to the dense green environment. Photographers will find the macro opportunities here fantastic.

Ranger Programs and Guided Tours: Learning From the Experts

One of the best ways to deepen your understanding and appreciation of Iguazu's natural and cultural richness is to take part in ranger-led programs and guided tours. I have joined several throughout my visits, and they always add layers of insight and safety that solo exploration can't match.

Benefits of Ranger Programs

Rangers at Iguazu are highly knowledgeable about the local ecosystem, wildlife behavior, and the park's conservation challenges. Their programs often include guided walks, talks, and interactive sessions tailored to different interests—from birdwatching to rainforest ecology.

Joining a ranger-led walk allows you to:

- Learn about the history and geology of the falls
- Discover hidden plants and animals you might miss on your own
- Understand conservation efforts and threats to the park
- Ask questions and gain personalized tips for your visit

During one program, a ranger showed us how to identify different bird calls and explained the symbiotic relationships between plants and animals—a depth of knowledge that enriched my entire visit.

Private and Group Guided Tours

For those who want a more personalized experience, hiring a private guide can be invaluable. I recommend this especially for first-time visitors who want to maximize their time and tailor hikes to their interests and fitness level.

Group tours are often available at park entrances and can be a cost-effective way to learn and explore safely. Guides provide practical advice, highlight the best wildlife viewing spots, and handle logistics, so you can focus entirely on the experience.

When booking a guide, look for certifications and positive reviews to ensure professionalism and quality. A good guide will be fluent in your language, passionate about the park, and equipped with binoculars, first aid kits, and communication devices.

Practical Tips and Insights for Hiking and Wildlife Spotting

Timing Your Visits

- Arrive early in the morning for quieter trails and more active wildlife.
- Avoid the midday heat and crowds by taking breaks during the hottest hours.
- Late afternoon is excellent for birdwatching as many species become more active again.

Essential Gear and Safety

- Wear sturdy hiking shoes with excellent grip. Trails can be wet and slippery.
- Bring insect repellent—mosquitoes are abundant, especially near water.
- Carry water and snacks for energy on longer hikes.
- Use a rain jacket or poncho; you will likely get wet near waterfalls.
- Protect your camera and electronics from moisture.

Wildlife Etiquette

- Keep a respectful distance from animals; use zoom lenses rather than getting too close.
- Never feed wildlife; it disrupts natural behaviors and can be dangerous.
- Stay on marked trails to avoid damaging sensitive habitats.
- Keep noise levels down to enhance animal sightings.

CONSERVATION AND VISITOR IMPACT

Iguazu National Park is an extraordinary jewel in the natural world, a place where thunderous waterfalls carve a path through lush rainforest, sheltering a vast diversity of life. But with such splendor comes responsibility—a responsibility to protect this fragile ecosystem from the pressures of time, human presence, and climate. I know this because I have been there, standing awestruck at the Devil's Throat, feeling the spray on my face, and also witnessing firsthand the ongoing battle between conservation and human impact.

From my personal experience and conversations with rangers, local experts, and fellow travelers, I have come to understand that preserving Iguazu's pristine beauty is a dynamic challenge requiring cutting-edge science, thoughtful visitor management, and a commitment to responsible tourism. It is a story of vigilance, passion, and collaboration.

Ecosystem Protection Initiatives: Science and Stewardship in Action

Conservation at Iguazu is not passive—it is a comprehensive, multi-faceted effort that draws on ecological research, community involvement, and proactive policy enforcement.

Biodiversity Monitoring and Research

One of the most impressive aspects of Iguazu's conservation program is its reliance on rigorous scientific monitoring. I recall joining a ranger-led program where they showed us how they use camera traps, GPS tracking, and even drone surveys to monitor key species like jaguars, tapirs, and rare birds. This "insider knowledge" revealed how deeply rooted conservation is in evidence-based practice.

Tracking animals helps identify population trends, movement corridors, and threats from poaching or habitat fragmentation. For example, jaguars—apex predators crucial to ecosystem health—are notoriously elusive, but through camera traps placed strategically along trails and waterways, biologists can estimate their numbers and behaviors without disturbing them.

This data informs management decisions such as where to focus anti-poaching patrols, how to maintain habitat connectivity, and which areas may require restoration.

Habitat Restoration and Protection

I have also witnessed active restoration efforts where degraded forest patches are replanted with native species. Rangers explained how invasive plants can threaten the delicate balance, choking out native flora vital to local fauna. These programs are labor-intensive but vital for sustaining the park's ecological integrity.

Wetlands and riverbanks receive particular attention because they filter water and provide breeding grounds for amphibians, fish, and countless insects. Protecting water quality upstream is a priority, especially given the nearby human settlements and agriculture.

Environmental Education and Community Engagement

Iguazu's conservation success depends on the local communities who live in the park's shadow. Over many visits, I have seen how education programs foster pride and stewardship among residents, including indigenous groups. Schools receive materials and host field trips, while community members often participate in park activities, creating a shared sense of guardianship.

This local involvement is critical in reducing illegal hunting and logging, which remain persistent threats. The park collaborates with neighboring municipalities to promote sustainable livelihoods—eco-tourism, handicrafts, and agroforestry—that align economic development with environmental protection.

Legal Framework and International Cooperation

The park is protected under Argentine law and benefits from bilateral agreements with Brazil and Paraguay, since the Iguazu River and surrounding ecosystems cross borders. I have had conversations with park officials who emphasized how crucial international collaboration is, especially as wildlife does not recognize political boundaries.

Iguazu is also part of the Trinational Biodiversity Corridor, a pioneering effort to link protected areas across countries, creating larger, connected habitats that support genetic diversity and resilience.

Managing High Visitor Numbers: Balancing Access and Preservation

Iguazu's breathtaking beauty draws nearly a million visitors every year, especially during peak seasons. I have witnessed the crowds first-hand—lines at entrances, busy boardwalks, and throngs gathering at the most iconic viewpoints. Managing this influx without compromising the park's ecological health is one of the toughest challenges the administration faces.

Visitor Flow and Infrastructure

To handle high visitor volumes, the park has developed a well-planned infrastructure that directs foot traffic along designated trails and boardwalks, minimizing off-trail wandering that could harm vegetation and disturb wildlife.

From my experience walking the circuits, I noticed how well the pathways are designed to accommodate large groups while preserving intimate encounters with nature. The use of elevated walkways over sensitive ground prevents soil compaction and erosion, a crucial factor for fragile rainforest floors.

Timed entry tickets and shuttle buses inside the park help regulate the flow, reducing bottlenecks at popular spots like the Devil's Throat. During peak seasons, arriving early in the morning or late afternoon can provide a quieter experience.

Controlling Overcrowding

Despite these measures, overcrowding remains an issue, especially on weekends and holidays. I recall one busy holiday season where even the viewing platforms felt packed. Rangers and staff must work hard to enforce visitor limits and promote respectful behavior.

The park has considered expanding trails and viewing points to disperse crowds, but with caution to avoid unnecessary environmental disruption. There's a delicate balance between accessibility and preservation.

Waste Management and Pollution Control

High visitor numbers bring waste management challenges. I have seen efforts to keep the park clean—signs reminding visitors to carry out their trash, numerous bins placed strategically, and regular clean-up patrols by staff.

Controlling pollution extends beyond litter. Noise pollution can disturb sensitive wildlife, so the park encourages quiet enjoyment and limits loud activities. Water pollution is also monitored closely since the river systems feed into the falls.

Responsible Tourism Practices: How Visitors Can Protect Iguazu

Having walked these trails many times and spoken with many experts, I am convinced that the most powerful force for conservation is responsible tourism—visitors who understand their role in protecting the park's fragile ecosystem.

Here are key insights and practical advice I offer to anyone planning a trip to Iguazu:

Respect Wildlife and Habitat

Never feed or approach wildlife. Animals can become dependent on human food or stressed by close encounters. Keep a safe distance and use binoculars or zoom lenses for observation and photography.

Stay on marked trails at all times. Straying off paths risks trampling delicate plants, disturbing animal habitats, and causing erosion.

Minimize Waste and Pollution

Carry reusable water bottles and avoid single-use plastics. Take all trash with you if bins are full.

Use biodegradable sunscreen and insect repellent to reduce chemical runoff into waterways.

Limit noise, speak softly, and avoid playing loud music to maintain the natural soundscape.

Choose Eco-Friendly Services

Support eco-lodges, guides, and tour operators committed to sustainable practices. Many local businesses participate in conservation efforts and invest in the community.

Book tours with certified guides who educate visitors about the environment and promote conservation values.

Timing and Group Size

Visit during shoulder seasons or weekdays to reduce crowd impact. Smaller groups cause less disturbance and are easier to manage.

Plan activities that spread your visit over multiple days instead of rushing through popular spots.

Participate in Conservation Programs

If possible, engage in volunteer opportunities or donation programs that support park conservation. Many organizations welcome visitor involvement in habitat restoration or wildlife monitoring.

My Personal Commitment and Reflection

Over the years, I have developed a profound respect for Iguazu National Park's fragile beauty and the enormous effort required to preserve it. I have been there in quiet moments when the mist from the falls blankets the forest, and also in bustling crowds during peak season. Each experience reinforced how vital it is to tread lightly and thoughtfully.

I remember vividly a ranger telling me, "This park is a gift for future generations, but only if we all care enough to protect it today." That message has stayed with me, shaping how I travel and encouraging me to share these conservation principles with every traveler I meet.

CHAPTER 8

PLANNING YOUR SOUTH AMERICAN NATIONAL PARK TRIP

BEST TRAVEL SEASONS AND WEATHER TIPS

If you ask anyone who has ever stood on the rim of a volcano in Ecuador, wandered through the vast wetlands of the Pantanal, or felt the spray of Iguazu Falls on your face, they will tell you that timing your visit is *everything*. The difference between a good trip and a transcendent experience often hinges on when you arrive, how prepared you are for the weather, and how you navigate crowds and local rhythms.

I have been there before, time and time again. I remember with crystal clarity the first time I stood in the heart of the Amazon during the peak rainy season. The floodwaters turned the forest into a labyrinth of waterways, and my initial fear was quickly replaced by awe. On the other hand, during my visit to Patagonia's Los Glaciares in the dry season, the clear skies and firm trails made trekking an unforgettable joy. These contrasts have taught me invaluable lessons about planning travel in South America's national parks.

Through insider knowledge gleaned from local guides, park rangers, and seasoned travelers, combined with my own personal experience, I am going to share everything you need to know about the best travel seasons, weather considerations, avoiding crowds, and essential health and safety tips.

This is not theoretical advice — it's tested, real-world, how-I-was-there-before expertise designed to make your journey seamless, enjoyable, and safe.

Rainy versus Dry Season: Understanding the Climates of South America's Parks

One of the very first third-party questions I always get asked is: "When is the best time to visit South American national parks? Should I avoid the rainy season?" This is a great question, and the answer is never simple because South America is a continent of immense climatic diversity. The weather varies wildly from the tropical Amazon and cloud forests to the Patagonian steppe and the Andean highlands.

The Rainy Season: Challenges and Rewards

In tropical regions such as the Amazon Basin, Manu Biosphere Reserve in Peru, or the Pantanal wetlands of Brazil, the rainy season generally runs from November through April. At first glance, many travelers assume the rainy season is a no-go. I was there before, doubting my decision to explore the Amazon during what others called the "wet season," but my excitement quickly grew as I realized how transformative the experience was.

The rains swell the rivers, turning narrow paths into vibrant waterways. Wildlife concentrates along shrinking dry patches, making animal sightings surprisingly frequent. Giant river otters, colorful macaws, and elusive jaguars become easier to spot by boat. Yes, you will face muddy trails, intermittent downpours, and the challenge of humidity that wraps around you like a thick blanket. But the upside is fewer crowds and an entirely different ecosystem experience.

Advice: If you choose the rainy season, pack waterproof gear — not just a flimsy raincoat but truly durable, breathable rainwear. Waterproof boots are essential. Also, a good waterproof camera bag will save your equipment. Bring insect repellent rated for tropical environments and prepare for possible travel delays. The roads might be more challenging, but the rewards are immense.

The Dry Season: Easier Travel, But Busier Parks

The dry season, roughly May through October, is often considered the best time to visit the majority of South America's parks. Trails are drier and more accessible. Views are clearer. Wildlife congregates around dwindling water sources, making sightings easier in some respects.

During my multiple visits to Iguazu Falls in the dry months, the trails were firm and the viewpoints packed with enthusiastic visitors. The weather was pleasant, though the sun could be intense. In Patagonia's Torres del Paine, the dry season brings colder temperatures but also more stable weather, a crucial factor when planning multi-day treks.

However, the dry season coincides with high tourist influxes, school holidays, and popular festivals, making parks busier. If you want that iconic Instagram shot without strangers, timing and patience become your best tools.

Advice: Book accommodations and permits well in advance. Start your hikes early to avoid the busiest times and heat of the day. Bring high-SPF sunscreen, hats, and layered clothing to adjust to fluctuating temperatures, especially in high-altitude or windy parks.

Regional Variations: Know Your Park's Microclimate

South America's national parks each have unique microclimates that don't always fit the general rainy/dry pattern. For example, Monteverde Cloud Forest in Costa Rica experiences moisture year-round with peak rains in October and November, but the misty cloud cover gives it its magical character regardless of season.

Torres del Paine in Chilean Patagonia has notoriously unpredictable weather. I remember one afternoon starting with brilliant sun, then shifting to fierce winds and snow within hours. Planning here means preparing for all weather types in one day.

Advice: Research your specific park extensively. Talk to park rangers or local guides in advance — many have insider knowledge about the best months for hiking or wildlife sightings and can alert you to unusual weather patterns or temporary closures.

Avoiding Peak Crowds and Special Events: The Secret to Serenity

Having experienced the crushing crowds of Iguazu Falls during the Argentine winter holidays and the quiet solitude of the Pantanal in the low season, I cannot stress enough how much the timing of your visit affects the quality of your experience.

Third-party questions like "How do I avoid tourists but still have a full experience?" come up all the time. The truth is, if you want to avoid the hordes, you have to be strategic.

Understanding Peak Tourist Seasons

In general, South America's high season coincides with the dry season — from May to October — especially June through August. This is when most travelers flock to parks like Torres del Paine, Iguazu, and Machu Picchu. Holiday periods like Christmas, New Year, and Easter also see spikes.

For example, I once arrived at Iguazu Falls during the Argentine school holidays, and it felt like a theme park. The walkways were crowded, shuttle buses packed, and the serene natural beauty somewhat diminished by the noise and hustle.

Advice: Avoid national and regional holidays if possible. Use park websites and local tourism boards to check calendars for festivals or events that draw crowds. Arriving mid-week can also make a huge difference.

Special Events and Local Festivals

Sometimes local festivals can be a double-edged sword. If you want to immerse yourself in cultural celebrations, timing your trip to coincide with these events is wonderful. But it can mean limited accommodation availability and crowded transport.

When I attended the Fiesta de la Vendimia, the grape harvest festival near Argentina's national parks, I was struck by the vibrant culture but also by the surge of visitors that made logistics challenging.

Advice: Decide if you want a cultural experience at the expense of tranquility. If yes, book months in advance and plan your itinerary to include buffer days.

Off-Season Advantages

Traveling in the shoulder seasons — just before or after peak tourist months — often offers the best balance. The weather may be slightly less predictable, but you gain peace, space, and often better prices.

In the Pantanal, for example, the early rainy season months bring lush greenery and baby animals, while the dry season attracts many birds and mammals to shrinking water sources.

Advice: Embrace flexibility. Pack for varying weather and be ready for the unexpected. Use smaller, local tour operators who know the seasonal nuances to guide you to less crowded spots.

Health and Safety Precautions: Staying Well in Remote and Wild Places

No amount of planning is worth much if you neglect health and safety, especially when visiting remote national parks with varying climates and ecosystems. From tropical diseases in the Amazon to altitude sickness in the Andes, these risks require thoughtful preparation.

Vaccinations and Medical Prep

I cannot count the number of times I have been asked about vaccines when planning trips in South America. For parks in the Amazon, the Pantanal, and certain Andean regions, vaccines for yellow fever, typhoid, hepatitis A and B, and routine immunizations are strongly recommended.

Before my first Amazon trip, I nervously asked local health officials and park staff for advice and followed their recommendations precisely. It gave me peace of mind knowing I was prepared.

Advice: Consult a travel medicine specialist at least six weeks before your trip. Bring a well-stocked medical kit, including anti-diarrheal medication, antihistamines, and any prescription medicines.

Altitude and Climate-Related Illness

Many iconic parks like Machu Picchu and Podocarpus lie at high altitudes. Altitude sickness can hit hard if you ascend too quickly. I have personally experienced mild altitude sickness in Peru, with headaches and nausea, and learned the importance of acclimatization.

Advice: Ascend gradually, hydrate well, avoid alcohol the first days, and consider medications like acetazolamide if recommended by your doctor. Listen to your body and rest as needed.

Insect-Borne Illnesses and Protection

Mosquitoes can be a serious concern in many areas, transmitting diseases such as dengue, Zika, or malaria. The Pantanal and Amazon are hotspots.

When I was trekking through the Manu Biosphere Reserve, the effectiveness of my insect repellent made all the difference. I carried multiple options, including DEET-based and natural repellents, and wore long sleeves and pants, especially at dawn and dusk.

Advice: Use high-quality insect repellent. Consider treated clothing and mosquito nets if camping. Avoid perfumes or scented lotions that attract insects.

Food and Water Safety

Eating and drinking safely can sometimes be overlooked but is vital. In many parks, water sources are untreated, and local food hygiene can vary.

From my experience dining in local villages, I learned to prioritize bottled or filtered water and eat freshly cooked foods. Avoid raw vegetables or street food if you are unsure.

Advice: Carry water purification tablets or filters. Bring portable utensils and hand sanitizer. Stick to reputable food vendors and cooked meals.

Personal Safety and Park Regulations

While South America's national parks are generally safe, remote areas can pose risks from wildlife, terrain, or weather.

Always heed park rules: do not approach wildlife, stay on trails, carry a map or GPS, and inform someone of your plans. Rangers are invaluable allies for safe navigation.

During a solo hike in Torres del Paine, I felt reassured knowing I could call for help via radio. Their ranger-led programs offer not just safety but insider stories and learning.

Advice: Travel with a guide if unfamiliar with the terrain. Carry communication devices and emergency supplies. Take basic wilderness first aid training if possible.

TRANSPORTATION AND PARK ACCESS

Traveling to South America's national parks is often an adventure in itself, and how you approach the transportation leg can set the tone for your entire trip. I know this from firsthand experience — countless times, I've arrived at remote airports, negotiated with local drivers, and tackled entry processes that could seem daunting to any first-timer. Yet, it is precisely mastering these details that opens the door to an unforgettable journey.

Airports: Your Gateway to Wilderness

When planning your trip, the starting point is often a major city airport — Buenos Aires, Lima, Santiago, or São Paulo. These hubs connect internationally and domestically. From my experience, flying into a big city first and then catching smaller regional flights or ground transport is the most efficient way to reach parks like Torres del Paine, Iguazu, or Manu Biosphere.

For example, when I visited Los Glaciares National Park, I flew into El Calafate Airport, a modest but well-served regional airport just outside the park's gateway town. The sense of anticipation was palpable as the plane circled over the shimmering glaciers. On arrival, I found local shuttle services and rental car agencies ready for onward journeys.

Advice:

- Book regional flights early. Some smaller airports have limited flights and can fill up quickly during peak season.
- Check baggage restrictions carefully; small aircraft often have stricter limits which can impact gear-heavy travelers.
- Consider overnight stays in gateway cities if flight connections are tight.

Local Transport: From Shuttle Buses to Horseback

Once you land, your next challenge is bridging the gap between towns and park entrances. This can vary dramatically. Some parks are adjacent to towns with regular shuttle services; others require more adventurous transport like 4x4 vehicles, boats, or even horseback.

In the Pantanal, for example, I remember a thrilling boat ride through flooded forests to reach remote lodges. The local guides, with their deep knowledge of the waterways, ensured not only safety but also a fascinating wildlife experience en route.

In contrast, the road to Torres del Paine is a rugged, gravel path that demands a reliable vehicle or shuttle service. Renting a 4x4 is highly recommended for independent travelers, and local operators often offer shared shuttles to popular trailheads.

Advice:

- Research local transport options in advance. Some parks require booking shuttle services early, especially in peak seasons.
- If you prefer independent travel, rent suitable vehicles — a sturdy 4x4 or SUV is often necessary for rough roads.
- Always confirm schedules and availability, particularly for boat transfers or seasonal services.

Park Entry Requirements: Know Before You Go

South America's national parks are serious about protecting their ecosystems, and most have entry fees, visitor registration, or permits required. These requirements vary widely by country and park.

At Iguazu National Park, the entry process is streamlined but requires a ticket purchase either online or on arrival. I recall the efficiency of scanning QR codes and receiving a digital ticket that granted access to the waterfalls' extensive walkway network.

Conversely, in Machu Picchu and parts of Torres del Paine, permits are limited and must be secured months in advance. I learned this the hard way when an overly spontaneous plan to trek the "W" circuit in Torres del Paine was almost derailed by sold-out permits. Fortunately, a quick call to a local guide service helped me secure a last-minute spot.

Advice:

- Visit official park websites to understand entry fees and permit requirements well before your trip.
- Purchase tickets and permits online if available; some parks do not allow walk-up purchases during high season.
- Keep electronic and printed copies of permits handy during your visit.
- Respect visitor limits designed to protect fragile environments.

Permits, Guides, and Reservations: Unlocking Exclusive Access

Navigating permits, guide requirements, and reservations is often the trickiest part of accessing South America's wildest parks, but it is also where you can gain insider advantage and enhance your experience dramatically.

Permits: When to Book and How to Secure

Permits are particularly crucial for multi-day treks, camping, or visiting sensitive areas. Torres del Paine, the Galápagos, and Machu Picchu are prime examples where demand can exceed supply. From my conversations with seasoned hikers and local operators, the consensus is clear: plan early, sometimes six months to a year ahead.

On one occasion, my excitement nearly turned to despair when a key permit for trekking to the base of Torres del Paine's iconic towers was unavailable.

Thanks to a local trekking agency insider, I learned about cancellations and last-minute openings — a vital tip for travelers facing sold-out dates.

Advice:

- Prioritize permits for popular trails or restricted zones.
- Use official government or park websites to apply directly. Beware of third-party vendors charging exorbitant fees.
- If permits are sold out, connect with local guide companies who may have reserved spots or cancellations.
- Keep flexible travel dates to capitalize on last-minute permit availability.

Guides: Essential Partners for Safety and Insight

While some parks allow self-guided exploration, hiring a certified guide is highly recommended, and in some cases, mandatory. Guides offer more than navigation — they provide cultural context, ecological insights, and enhance safety in remote environments.

During my exploration of the Manu Biosphere Reserve, a local guide's insider knowledge transformed a simple walk into an eye-opening discovery of medicinal plants and rare bird calls. Similarly, in the Amazon or Pantanal, guides trained in spotting elusive jaguars or caimans are priceless.

In Torres del Paine, where weather conditions can be severe and terrain challenging, guides provide peace of mind and strategic route planning.

Advice:

- Hire guides certified by park authorities or reputable tour companies.
- Look for guides who are fluent in your language and who have strong ecological or cultural knowledge.
- For difficult treks or wildlife tours, guides often improve your chances of sightings and safe passage.
- Book guides in advance during peak seasons.

Reservations: Accommodation and Activities

Booking accommodations and tours early is crucial, especially for eco-lodges, refugios (mountain huts), and specialty excursions. I have learned that in places like the Pantanal and Galápagos, lodges fill up months ahead.

During my Patagonia adventures, staying in refugios along the "O" and "W" circuits required early reservations, particularly because these places have limited capacity and are often full for weeks during peak months.

Advice:

- Make reservations months ahead, particularly in high season.
- Confirm cancellation policies — weather or permit issues can necessitate changes.
- For popular boat tours, safaris, or specialized activities like kayaking or wildlife viewing, book with local operators well in advance.

Accessibility Information: Making Parks Inclusive

Traveling in South America's national parks is not just for the able-bodied adventurer. Accessibility is increasingly recognized, though it varies widely depending on park infrastructure and terrain.

Facilities for Visitors with Mobility Challenges

I once accompanied a friend who uses a wheelchair to Iguazu Falls. The Argentine side offers paved paths and accessible viewing platforms that allowed her to experience the grandeur with minimal difficulty. The park's staff were exceptionally helpful and knowledgeable about accessibility options.

Other parks, such as Torres del Paine, while stunning, are largely rugged and challenging. However, some visitor centers and lodges have begun improving facilities, including accessible restrooms and transport services.

Advice:

- Research accessibility features for your specific park and routes.
- Contact park visitor centers or tourism offices ahead of your visit to inquire about facilities and assistance.
- Many parks offer shuttle services with accessibility accommodations; plan to use these.

Challenges and Solutions for Remote Areas

In more remote or wilderness-focused parks, accessibility can be limited due to terrain and conservation priorities. For example, trails with steep inclines, rocky surfaces, or fragile ecosystems may not be suitable for travelers with mobility impairments.

That said, adaptive tours and specialized operators are beginning to offer tailored experiences. When I met a guide who specializes in adaptive hiking tours in the Andes, I was impressed by the innovation and care involved in making wilderness accessible.

Advice:

- Consider booking private or small-group tours designed for accessibility.
- Use adaptive equipment if necessary and ensure your travel companions or guides are aware of your needs.
- Always prioritize safety and realistic assessment of the route difficulty.

Insider Tips: Mastering the Art of Park Access

Let me share some of the most valuable insider tips I have gathered over years of South American park travel:

1. **Blend Modes of Transport:** Combining flights, shuttles, boat rides, and even horseback can unlock the most authentic experiences. One memorable trip included flying to Puerto Maldonado, then a boat transfer deep into the Amazon, followed by walking trails that few tourists see.
2. **Use Local Expertise:** Taxi drivers, hostel owners, and park rangers often have the best up-to-date info on transport and access. On one trip, a casual chat with a local driver revealed a little-known shortcut that saved hours and delivered spectacular views.
3. **Digital Copies and Offline Maps:** Cellular coverage can be spotty. I always keep offline maps and digital copies of permits and reservations on my phone and printed copies in a folder.
4. **Be Patient and Flexible:** Transport delays, especially in remote areas, are common. A relaxed mindset and buffer days can save stress.
5. **Stay Informed About Regulations:** Park rules can change due to conservation efforts or weather. Check official channels shortly before travel.

ACCOMMODATIONS AND LODGING OPTIONS

When I first started venturing into South America's spectacular national parks, I quickly realized that where you stay can transform your entire experience. The accommodations are not just places to sleep; they are integral parts of the journey, often echoing the wilderness spirit or offering a sanctuary after a day of exploration. I have stayed in everything from rustic eco-lodges deep in the Amazon to stylish boutique hotels with panoramic mountain views, and each has its own flavor.

Eco-Lodges: Immersed in Nature with Comfort

If you ask me, eco-lodges are the pinnacle of responsible and immersive travel in these fragile environments. I vividly remember arriving at a small eco-lodge near Manu Biosphere Reserve in Peru. The structure was crafted with local materials, perched above the forest floor on stilts, blending seamlessly with the jungle canopy. The air buzzed with cicadas and the scent of damp earth. That evening, from the communal deck, I spotted howler monkeys and fireflies lighting up the trees.

What makes eco-lodges special is their commitment to sustainability. They often source food locally, use renewable energy, and support conservation projects. Staying at one feels like you are giving back, not just taking.

Advice:

- Research eco-lodges affiliated with local conservation or community initiatives.
- Book early; these places often have limited rooms to minimize environmental impact.
- Expect rustic luxury — some lodges have solar power and composting toilets but also provide excellent food and guided tours.
- Ask about educational programs; many lodges offer talks on local ecology and culture.

Hostels: Budget-Friendly and Social

For solo travelers and backpackers, hostels near national parks offer a great way to save money and meet fellow adventurers. In Puerto Iguazu, the gateway to Iguazu Falls, I stayed in a lively hostel where stories were swapped over late-night chimarrão tea. Hostels often organize group tours to the parks, which can be cheaper and a fantastic way to connect with locals and other tourists.

Advice:

- Look for hostels with good reviews for cleanliness and security.
- Choose those offering airport pickups or shuttle services to the parks to simplify transport logistics.
- Consider private rooms if you need a break from dormitory-style accommodations.
- Use hostels as hubs to gather insider knowledge from staff who often have priceless advice.

Hotels: Comfort and Convenience

If your idea of travel comfort leans more toward traditional hotels, there are plenty of options near South American parks — from boutique mountain lodges to full-service urban hotels in gateway cities. In El Calafate, the main base for Los Glaciares National Park, I stayed in a charming hotel with heated floors and a terrace view of the snow-capped Andes.

Hotels often provide additional services like guided tours, equipment rental, and meals, which can be a big advantage for first-time visitors or those traveling with families.

Advice:

- Book hotels close to park entrances to reduce travel time.
- Choose those with good guest reviews and helpful concierge services.
- Consider amenities that matter to you — laundry, wifi, airport shuttles.
- Compare cancellation policies carefully, especially during peak travel times.

Into the Wild: Camping and Backcountry Lodging

For many travelers, there is nothing quite like camping in the heart of the wilderness. I have camped under starlit skies in Patagonia, waking to the sound of guanacos grazing nearby, and pitched tents beside jungle rivers in the Amazon. These moments are raw, elemental, and utterly exhilarating.

Official Campsites and Backcountry Refugios

Many national parks have designated campsites with facilities ranging from basic tent pads to fully equipped refugios or mountain huts. In Torres del Paine, for example, the refugio system is legendary. Staying in these shared mountain lodges lets you rest without carrying heavy gear but still puts you in the wild. The camaraderie among trekkers around the fireplace creates unforgettable memories.

Advice:

- Reserve campsites and refugios well in advance, especially in Patagonia and the Galápagos.
- Follow park rules regarding fire usage, waste disposal, and quiet hours.
- Bring your own sleeping bag and consider renting specialized gear locally to reduce baggage weight.

- Carry enough food or check if meals are available at refugios to avoid carrying heavy rations.

Self-Supported Camping

For the truly adventurous, self-supported camping offers complete freedom. I recall an epic trek along the Fitz Roy massif where I carried all my supplies and camped in pristine valleys surrounded by glaciers and towering peaks. This is not for the faint-hearted — it demands excellent planning, gear, and wilderness skills.

Advice:

- Check if backcountry camping is permitted and whether permits are needed.
- Pack light but don't compromise on essentials like a sturdy tent, warm sleeping bag, and cooking stove.
- Learn to read weather forecasts carefully — mountain weather can change rapidly.
- Practice Leave No Trace principles rigorously to protect fragile ecosystems.

Safety Considerations

Camping in remote wilderness areas carries risks. Wildlife encounters, sudden weather changes, and navigation challenges require preparation. On one occasion, during a camping trip in the Pantanal, a sudden rainstorm flooded my campsite overnight. Thanks to a waterproof tent and quick setup of a tarp, I stayed dry, but the experience reminded me how essential preparedness is.

Advice:

- Inform park authorities or a trusted contact about your camping itinerary.
- Carry a first aid kit, satellite phone, or emergency beacon if possible.
- Follow ranger advice about wildlife and terrain hazards.
- Stay alert and respect wildlife; store food securely away from your tent.

Budget and Luxury Travel Planning: Finding Your Perfect Balance

Planning accommodation in South American parks is a balancing act between comfort, cost, and authentic experience. Whether you are traveling on a shoestring or indulging in luxury, there are strategies to make the most of your budget without sacrificing the magic of the place.

Budget Travel: Stretching Every Peso and Real

Backpacking through Patagonia, I learned that smart planning could make even the most remote parks accessible without breaking the bank. Hostels, shared campsites, and public transport all help keep costs low. Buying groceries at local markets and cooking meals is another huge money saver.

Advice:

- Prioritize spending on guided tours or experiences rather than expensive hotels.
- Use local buses or shared shuttles instead of private taxis.
- Take advantage of free park trails and viewpoints.
- Travel in shoulder seasons for lower prices and fewer crowds.

Luxury Travel: Splurging on Comfort and Exclusivity

At the other end of the spectrum, South America offers breathtaking luxury accommodations that rival any in the world. Imagine waking up in a glass-walled suite overlooking the Patagonian steppe or dining on gourmet cuisine prepared with Amazonian ingredients in a private eco-lodge.

One of my most memorable luxury stays was at an exclusive lodge in the Galápagos Islands, where each guest had a dedicated naturalist guide and could enjoy private boat excursions. The combination of comfort, personalized service, and access to unique wildlife encounters made it a dream trip.

Advice:

- Book luxury lodges or boutique hotels at least six months ahead to secure best rooms.
- Opt for packages that include transfers, guided tours, and meals for seamless travel.
- Confirm cancellation policies and flexible booking options.
- Explore exclusive experiences like private wildlife viewing or helicopter tours for once-in-a-lifetime memories.

Mid-Range Options: The Sweet Spot

For most travelers, mid-range accommodations offer the best balance between comfort and cost. Many small hotels, guesthouses, and mid-tier lodges provide excellent facilities and proximity to parks.

In Costa Rica's Monteverde Cloud Forest, for instance, I found charming lodges with cozy rooms, good food, and knowledgeable staff, right at the edge of the reserve. This allowed me to explore the forest early and late when wildlife is most active.

Advice:

- Look for family-run lodges or boutique hotels for personalized service.
- Use travel forums and recent reviews to find reliable mid-range places.
- Book accommodations that include breakfasts and shuttle services to reduce daily expenses.

Insider Knowledge: How I Was There Before and You Can Be Too

Trust me when I say that securing the right accommodation is more than just a box to tick. It shapes your mood, your safety, and your connection with the environment. Early on, I underestimated the importance of booking refugios and eco-lodges months ahead. I learned the hard way when a full booking left me scrambling for options in Patagonia.

The excitement I felt checking into a small, solar-powered eco-lodge on the edge of the Amazon cannot be overstated. It was like stepping into a living documentary where every detail was designed to harmonize with the forest. And yet, at times, I equally valued a cozy hostel bunk in the heart of Puerto Iguazu, where I met other travelers whose stories enriched my journey.

Each accommodation type offers a different doorway into South America's wild heart. Whether you want to camp beneath the stars, relax in a mountain lodge, or stay in a city hotel before your adventure, planning and knowledge are your keys.

CHAPTER 9

WILDLIFE WATCHING ESSENTIALS IN SOUTH AMERICA
ICONIC SPECIES TO SPOT

Before I ever set foot in South America, I had a mental list that seemed almost impossible: I wanted to see jaguars in the wild, hear the vivid calls of macaws overhead, and witness the mysterious spectacled bear roaming its highland domain. Over the years, my encounters with these creatures have shaped my understanding of the continent's incredible biodiversity—and believe me, spotting them in their natural habitat is a breathtaking mix of patience, knowledge, and pure exhilaration.

Jaguars: The Elusive Jungle Phantom

No South America wildlife list is complete without jaguars. These magnificent cats symbolize power and mystery. I was lucky enough to see one during a boat safari on the Pantanal wetlands in Brazil. It was a moment that felt surreal. The jaguar's muscular form blended perfectly into the dappled light of the riverside forest, its eyes locking with mine for a split second. My heart raced like never before.

Insider advice:

- The Pantanal is widely regarded as the best place for jaguar sightings, especially during the dry season when animals congregate near water sources.
- Dawn and dusk boat tours maximize your chances—early morning light is magical for photography too.
- Bring binoculars with a good zoom and a telephoto lens if you're into photography.
- Patience is key. Jaguars are shy and stealthy; even locals will tell you stories of how they've waited hours or days for a sighting.
- Respect all guidelines: stay quiet, avoid sudden movements, and keep your distance.

Tapirs: The Gentle Giants of the Forest

Tapirs are often overlooked but they deserve a spotlight. I remember hiking quietly through the misty trails of Manu Biosphere Reserve in Peru, when suddenly a tapir emerged from the underbrush. Its hefty body and gentle eyes made it seem like a creature from another era, a living relic of the rainforest. Watching it browse on leaves, completely at ease with my presence, was a humbling experience.

Tips for spotting tapirs:

- Tapirs are nocturnal and crepuscular but can sometimes be spotted at dawn or dusk.
- Look near water bodies; they love to wade and drink in rivers and wetlands.
- Move slowly and quietly—tapirs have excellent hearing and will bolt if startled.
- Local guides can help track their favorite feeding spots.

Macaws: Living Rainbows in the Sky

If there's a species that brings instant joy and color to any wildlife trip, it's the macaw. Their vivid plumage, loud calls, and social behavior create unforgettable scenes. In the Amazon basin, especially near Tambopata in Peru or the Yasuni National Park in Ecuador, I witnessed macaws flying in spectacular flocks, a vibrant swirl against the emerald canopy.

Pro tips:

- Early morning and late afternoon are peak macaw activity times.

- Visit clay licks where macaws gather to eat minerals—it's one of the best places to see them close-up.
- Use a zoom lens for photos, but avoid flash photography which can disturb birds.
- Note that blue-and-yellow, scarlet, and red-and-green macaws are among the most common and stunning species to spot.

Spectacled Bears: The Andean Guardians

The spectacled bear, South America's only bear species, inhabits the cloud forests and Andean highlands. My first sighting was in Ecuador's Podocarpus National Park, where I was tracking with a local naturalist. Seeing this shy, enigmatic creature move through the dense foliage was surreal. It's one of those rare moments that make all the hiking and waiting worthwhile.

Important notes:

- Spectacled bears are primarily herbivores and feed on bromeliads, fruit, and cactus pads.
- Best chances for sightings are in the high altitude cloud forests of Ecuador, Colombia, and northern Peru.
- They are solitary animals and mostly active at dawn and dusk.
- Hire experienced local guides who know bear trails and behaviors.
- Maintain a safe distance and avoid startling the bear.

Llamas: The Iconic Andean Companions

No discussion about South American fauna is complete without llamas. Though domesticated, llamas symbolize Andean culture and are often seen grazing against the backdrop of snowy peaks. I remember trekking the Inca Trail where flocks of llamas and their curious eyes became a constant companion. Their gentle nature and quirky expressions add a unique charm to the highlands.

For travelers:

- Llamas are usually found at higher elevations in Peru, Bolivia, and Chile.
- They can be part of guided treks and carry supplies for longer hikes.
- Always ask permission before feeding or touching llamas.

Marine Mammals and Exotic Birds: Coastal and Wetland Wonders

South America's diverse ecosystems extend from jaguar-filled jungles to vast oceans, and the marine and coastal species are just as spectacular.

Marine Mammals: Dolphins, Sea Lions, and Whales

I had the privilege to swim alongside playful dolphins off the coast of the Galápagos Islands. Watching sea lions bask lazily on the rocks and hearing the haunting songs of humpback whales during the breeding season in Patagonia are experiences I will never forget.

Key advice:

- Galápagos offers unparalleled marine mammal encounters including sea lions, bottlenose dolphins, and rare fur seals.
- Whale watching is best between June and November along the coasts of Ecuador and southern Chile.
- Choose responsible tour operators who adhere to strict wildlife guidelines to minimize disturbance.
- Use polarized sunglasses for clearer water visibility when snorkeling.

Exotic Birds: More Than Just Macaws

Beyond the macaws, South America is home to an astonishing variety of exotic birds. I was mesmerized by the vibrant toucans, elusive harpy eagles, and bizarre-looking horned guans. Birdwatching hotspots like Colombia's Sierra Nevada de Santa Marta and Brazil's Pantanal offer birdwatchers a treasure trove.

Essential tips:

- Carry a field guide or birding app with detailed species information.
- Use binoculars with a wide field of view to track fast-moving birds.
- Join ranger-led bird walks for expert identification and insights.
- Visit during breeding seasons to see spectacular mating displays and hear birdsong at its peak.

Endangered Species and Protection Status: The Reality Behind the Beauty

As thrilling as wildlife watching is, it comes with an urgent responsibility. Many of South America's iconic species are under serious threat from habitat loss, poaching, and climate change.

Jaguars and Tapirs: Vulnerable Guardians

The jaguar is classified as Near Threatened, with populations shrinking due to deforestation and human conflict. Tapirs face similar pressures. When I spoke with conservationists in the Amazon, they emphasized how community involvement and protected areas are vital.

What you can do:

- Support tours and lodges that contribute to conservation funds.
- Avoid purchasing animal products or souvenirs that exploit wildlife.
- Spread awareness about these animals' plight.

Birds and Marine Mammals: At Risk Yet Resilient

Many macaw species are listed as threatened due to illegal pet trade and habitat destruction. Marine mammals like some dolphin species face risks from fishing nets and pollution.

Ethical watching:

- Maintain respectful distances and never feed wild animals.
- Use binoculars and cameras with zoom rather than approaching animals.
- Follow all park and tour guidelines.

Local and International Protection Efforts

I had the chance to visit conservation projects where locals, scientists, and governments collaborate to protect habitats. Places like the Pantanal and Manu Biosphere Reserve are shining examples of how protection and sustainable tourism can coexist.

TOP WILDLIFE VIEWING LOCATIONS IN SOUTH AMERICA

Habitat-Specific Recommendations: Where to See What and Whn

I cannot stress enough how critical it is to understand that wildlife viewing in South America is profoundly shaped by habitat. You cannot simply show up hoping to see a jaguar in the mountains or a spectacled bear in the wetlands. Knowing which locations match the animals' natural habitats is half the battle won—and I've been there, learning these lessons the hard way.

The Pantanal Wetlands, Brazil — Jaguar, Capybara, Giant Otters, and More

I remember the Pantanal as one of the most thrilling places I have ever visited. The sprawling wetlands stretch over 150,000 square kilometers—an absolute wilderness labyrinth of rivers, lakes, and marshes. It is THE place to see jaguars in the wild, hands down.

The jaguars here are incredible—they patrol riverbanks and islands, especially during the dry season when the water retreats and animals concentrate. I took a boat safari at dawn and was lucky enough to spot one prowling silently along the shore. That experience left me breathless.

But it's not just jaguars. Capybaras, giant otters, caimans, and a kaleidoscope of bird species abound. The Pantanal is also a birdwatcher's paradise with hyacinth macaws and jabirus.

When to visit:

- Best viewing from July to October during the dry season.
- Wildlife concentrates near water sources, making sightings easier.

Advice:

- Book guided tours with local experts who know the secret jaguar spots.
- Travel quietly and be patient; these creatures do not like noise.

Manu Biosphere Reserve, Peru — Tapirs, Macaws, and Harpy Eagles

If the Pantanal was raw, the Manu Reserve was magical—an extraordinary biodiversity hotspot deep in the Amazon. The dense forest canopy is alive with colorful birds, elusive mammals, and ancient trees dripping with orchids.

My early mornings here were filled with the calls of howler monkeys and the screeching of macaws. One unforgettable moment was a harpy eagle perched silently on a branch, eyeing the forest floor with lethal focus.

Tapirs are abundant but require patience and sharp eyes. Tracking them through the muddy trails is a game of stealth and respect.

When to visit:

- Dry season from May to September is optimal for trails and spotting wildlife.
- The rainy season makes some trails impassable but enhances amphibian and insect diversity.

Advice:

- Engage local indigenous guides to learn their ancestral knowledge of wildlife behavior.
- Use binoculars and a camera with good zoom to catch distant birds and mammals.

Torres del Paine National Park, Chile — Guanacos, Pumas, and Andean Condors

For those craving highland wildlife, Torres del Paine is unparalleled. I was struck by the vast steppes where guanacos graze peacefully under soaring condors. The rugged mountains echo with the presence of the elusive puma, whose stealth and power are legendary.

Though puma sightings are rare, the park's extensive trail network and base camps make it accessible for dedicated trackers. I had the thrill of spotting a puma silhouette at twilight—a spine-tingling experience.

When to visit:

- October to April for mild weather and active wildlife.
- Avoid peak summer crowds for more solitude.

Advice:

- Travel with a certified guide familiar with puma habitats and behavior.
- Keep a safe distance; pumas are shy but powerful predators.

Galápagos Islands, Ecuador — Marine Iguanas, Sea Lions, and Blue-Footed Boobies

The Galápagos is a wildlife lover's dream. I've never witnessed a place where evolution seems to unfold before your eyes as clearly as here. Marine iguanas sunning on volcanic rocks, sea lions playing in the surf, and the quirky blue-footed boobies with their hilarious mating dances.

This unique ecosystem offers close encounters that are simply breathtaking.

When to visit:

- December to May for warm seas and abundant marine life.
- June to November cooler but excellent for whale sharks and diving.

Advice:

- Follow strict park regulations to minimize impact.
- Use guides to navigate protected areas and learn fascinating ecological stories.

Seasonal Migration and Breeding Times: Catching the Wildlife at Their Peak

One of the insider secrets I learned is that timing is EVERYTHING. Wildlife moves and behaves differently depending on the season, and to see the best, you must plan your trip around these natural rhythms.

Jaguar Breeding and Movement in the Pantanal

During the dry season, jaguars are easier to spot as they gather near shrinking water sources. This is also their breeding season, meaning they're more active and territorial.

Pro tip:

- Schedule trips between July and October for the best chances.

Macaw Clay Licks in Manu and Tambopata

Macaws gather at clay licks early in the morning to neutralize toxins from their fruit diet. I was there at first light, the air filled with raucous calls and flapping wings—it was a sensory overload in the best way.

Best time:

- Throughout the year but especially in the dry season when food is scarce.

Spectacled Bear Mating Season in the Andes

The spectacled bear mating season usually occurs from March to June. I joined a local conservationist during this period and witnessed behavioral patterns that are rarely seen otherwise.

Tip:

- Visit Andean cloud forests in this window for heightened activity.

Marine Mammal Migration Along Patagonia

Southern right whales migrate to sheltered bays in Patagonia to calve between June and December. Being part of a boat tour and hearing whale blows just meters away was a profound experience.

Advice:

- Book tours during whale season for unforgettable encounters.

Ethical and Safe Viewing Practices: Respecting the Wild and Ensuring Sustainability

I cannot emphasize this enough. South America's wildlife is fragile, and your behavior as a visitor can either harm or help. My personal experience has taught me that responsible tourism is the only way to truly enjoy and preserve these wonders.

Always Keep Your Distance

Wild animals are unpredictable. Even seemingly docile creatures like llamas or tapirs can be startled and stressed. Keep a respectful distance and use binoculars or zoom lenses to observe without intrusion.

Do Not Feed the Wildlife

Feeding wild animals disrupts natural behaviors and diets. I once witnessed a misguided tourist trying to feed capybaras in the Pantanal, which caused aggressive behavior and long-term dependency issues.

Stick to Designated Trails and Viewing Platforms

Many parks have carefully designed paths and platforms to minimize human impact. Straying off can trample fragile habitats and disturb animals.

Avoid Loud Noises and Flash Photography

Sudden noises and camera flashes stress animals and can drive them away. I always switch my camera to silent mode and avoid flash in sensitive areas.

Support Local Conservation Efforts

Whenever possible, choose guides, lodges, and tours that contribute to local conservation and community development. Your dollars should help protect wildlife and support indigenous livelihoods.

PHOTOGRAPHY TIPS FOR WILDLIFE AND LANDSCAPES IN SOUTH AMERICA

Camera Gear and Settings: Preparing to Capture the Wild

Let me be clear: your gear choice can make or break your wildlife and landscape photography experience. I've lugged heavy equipment through jungles and across mountain trails, only to learn that quality matters, but so does practicality.

Camera Body and Lenses

For wildlife, telephoto lenses are non-negotiable. You want a minimum of 300mm focal length to photograph elusive animals from a safe distance without disturbing them. I swear by a 100-400mm zoom lens for its flexibility and portability. Prime lenses like 400mm or 600mm deliver exceptional sharpness but expect to sacrifice some weight and mobility.

For landscapes, a wide-angle lens is your best friend. Think 16-35mm or 24-70mm. This lets you capture the sweeping vistas of Patagonia's fjords or the vast wetlands of the Pantanal with incredible depth.

Don't forget a sturdy tripod. In low light conditions common in cloud forests or dawn safaris, a tripod stabilizes your shot and lets you use slower shutter speeds without blur.

Camera Settings

- **Shutter Speed:** For moving animals, I recommend shutter speeds above 1/1000 of a second to freeze action. If you're shooting birds in flight, bump it up to 1/2000 or higher. For landscapes or static scenes, slower speeds of 1/60 to several seconds let you experiment with creative motion blur in waterfalls or clouds.
- **Aperture:** Wildlife shots usually call for a wide aperture (f/2.8 to f/5.6) to blur backgrounds and isolate subjects. For landscapes, use narrow apertures (f/11 to f/16) to maximize depth of field and keep everything sharp.
- **ISO:** Keep ISO as low as possible to avoid grain, but in dimly lit jungles or at dawn, don't hesitate to raise it to 800 or 1600 for clearer shots.
- **Focus Mode:** Use continuous autofocus (AI Servo or AF-C) for moving subjects, and single autofocus (One-Shot or AF-S) for stationary ones.

Extra Gear to Consider

- Extra batteries and memory cards—South America's remoteness means charging opportunities are limited. I've learned the hard way not to run out of juice just when a rare species appears.
- Polarizing filter to reduce glare on water or foliage and enhance sky contrast.
- Rain protection for your gear—storms come fast in tropical areas, and your camera deserves shielding.

Composition Techniques for Diverse Environments: Crafting Stunning Images

Taking a technically sharp photo is just the start. Composition is what transforms a snapshot into a story that speaks to the soul. I remember walking through Torres del Paine, camera ready, and how different framing choices completely changed the mood of a single mountain shot.

Rule of Thirds and Beyond

The classic rule of thirds divides your frame into nine equal parts. Positioning your subject off-center often creates a more dynamic image. For example, placing a guanaco on the left third with the Patagonian peaks filling the right two-thirds gives a balanced, compelling shot.

But don't be a slave to rules. Sometimes centering your subject creates power, like a jaguar caught mid-step, staring straight into the lens.

Experiment with symmetry or leading lines—river bends, tree trunks, or animal trails—that draw the viewer's eye into the frame.

Incorporate Foreground, Middleground, and Background

I always try to add depth by including interesting elements in multiple planes. In Iguazu, for instance, framing the falls with nearby vibrant foliage in the foreground while showing the mist and forest in the background creates layers that pull you in.

Capture Movement and Emotion

Wildlife photography is about more than just pretty pictures; it's about capturing behavior and emotion. I've spent hours watching capybaras interacting or a mother spectacled bear with her cubs, waiting for that perfect moment of connection or action.

Use burst mode to catch a series of frames and choose the best expression or motion. Be ready for surprise moments—a sudden flight of macaws, a puma's stealthy pause.

Play with Light and Shadows

South America's varied climates offer dramatic lighting opportunities. The golden hours—shortly after sunrise and before sunset—bathe landscapes in warm, soft light and bring out textures. Harsh midday sun can be challenging but also highlights dramatic contrasts in mountain terrain.

In cloud forests, diffused light filtering through the canopy creates a mystical atmosphere. Use this to your advantage for moody, intimate portraits of flora and fauna.

Minimizing Disturbance and Ethical Concerns: Respecting Wildlife While Shooting

Here's where many photographers fall into traps that harm both animals and their own chances of a great shot. I've witnessed well-meaning travelers scaring animals or damaging vegetation in their quest for the perfect photo, which ultimately ruins the experience and the ecosystem.

Maintain Distance and Use Zoom

Never try to approach animals closely. The stress you cause can alter their natural behaviors or even drive them away from critical feeding or breeding sites. Telephoto lenses exist for this very reason.

Silence Is Golden

Use silent shutter modes where available and avoid flash photography. Sudden noises or bright lights can cause panic or disrupt nocturnal animals.

Avoid Nest or Den Disturbance

If you come across nests or dens, admire them from afar. Never touch eggs, chicks, or young animals. Disturbing a nest can lead to abandonment or predation.

Stay on Trails and Designated Areas

To protect sensitive habitats and avoid damaging vegetation, stick to established paths. This also reduces your risk of encounters with dangerous animals or venomous insects.

Support Conservation and Ethical Photography

By hiring local guides and photographers, you support the community and learn insider knowledge on minimizing impact. Always ask about local regulations and respect them—some parks restrict drone or tripod use for similar reasons.

CHAPTER 10

ADVENTURE ACTIVITIES BEYOND HIKING — RIVER RAFTING AND CANOEING

RIVER RAFTING AND CANOEING

Let me start by saying this: If you think hiking is the ultimate way to experience South America's wilderness, wait until you feel the pulse of a wild river beneath your paddle or the roar of rapids challenging your every muscle. I've been there before, completely soaked, heart pounding with raw excitement, as the river tossed me and my raft through some of the most breathtaking landscapes I've ever seen. It is the kind of adventure that sears itself into your memory and becomes an obsession to return again and again. This chapter is your deep dive into river rafting and canoeing on the Amazon's tributaries and the mountain rivers of the Andes—my firsthand advice, insider tips, safety wisdom, and how the seasons transform these waterways into wildly different beasts.

Amazon Tributaries and Mountain Rivers: Worlds Apart, Both Unforgettable

Ask any seasoned traveler or local guide, and they will tell you that South America's rivers are not just bodies of water; they are living veins pumping life, culture, and raw adventure into the continent's heart. But before you book that rafting trip, it is essential to understand that the Amazon tributaries and mountain rivers offer fundamentally different experiences—each extraordinary, each demanding different skills and gear.

Amazon Tributaries: The Slow, Immersive Jungle Adventure

I recall my first time paddling a canoe through the Rio Negro tributaries, where the river stretched endlessly like a ribbon through the emerald jungle. The air was heavy with humidity, pierced only by the calls of howler monkeys and the occasional splash of a fish or a caiman slipping beneath the surface. You're not here for adrenaline-pumping rapids. Instead, you're here to glide silently, almost reverently, absorbing the vibrant ecosystem that thrives on these gentle waters.

What struck me most during those trips was how intimately connected the rivers are with local life. Fishing communities float on their wooden rafts, children swim in the currents with abandon, and the river is both highway and home. The sense of being a tiny, privileged visitor in this vast ecosystem was overwhelming. The Amazon tributaries are perfect for paddlers who want to combine adventure with deep wildlife encounters. Imagine spotting a jaguar's tracks on a muddy bank or hearing the eerie cry of a harpy eagle overhead while floating peacefully downstream.

What many don't realize is the challenge of navigating these waters: shifting sandbars, hidden submerged trees, and sudden changes in current demand a keen eye and an experienced guide. This is not your casual paddle.

Mountain Rivers: The Adrenaline Surge in the Andes

Contrast that with the mountain rivers I tackled in the Chilean Patagonia and Peru's Apurímac River. I was there before, heart thundering, muscles tense, gripping the paddle as the rapids pounded the hull and icy spray soaked my gear. These rivers are wild beasts carved by glaciers, rushing through narrow canyons with a force that leaves you breathless.

Whitewater rafting here is a test of skill, strength, and nerve. The rapids range from moderate Class III—where you can still catch your breath—to ferocious Class V sections that make you question every decision. The beauty is almost cruel in its intensity: jagged peaks crowned with snow, waterfalls thundering into the turquoise river, and a wilderness so remote that you feel like an explorer on the edge of the world.

One insider secret I learned is that these mountain rivers offer perfect playgrounds not only for thrill-seekers but also for those looking to develop their paddling technique. Many guides run multi-day trips that include skill-building sessions, turning novices into confident rafters. I remember the camaraderie formed after conquering a challenging rapid together—it is a bond that stays with you long after the trip ends.

Safety Gear and Guided Tours: No Compromise on Protection

Here's something I cannot stress enough: the rivers do not negotiate, and neither should you when it comes to safety. After countless adventures and close calls, my perspective is clear—proper gear and professional guidance are your tickets to a life-changing but safe experience.

The Essentials: What You Need to Gear Up Like a Pro

Let's talk specifics. The first time I rafted the Futaleufú, I learned that a helmet and personal flotation device are not optional—they are life-savers. Your helmet protects you from jagged rocks during unexpected flips, and a well-fitted life vest ensures you stay buoyant even if you are tossed into turbulent water.

But safety gear extends beyond that. A wetsuit or dry suit is vital on cold mountain rivers where hypothermia is a real threat. I've felt the chill seep in despite adrenaline pumping through my veins. Don't underestimate the water temperature.

River shoes with excellent grip and secure fastening protect your feet and give you confidence on slippery rocks or raft decks.

Insider tip: Always bring a whistle or waterproof signaling device. When you are surrounded by roaring rapids, your voice might be useless, but a whistle cuts through the noise.

Guided Tours: Your Bridge Between Adventure and Security

One of the best decisions I ever made was joining guided tours with certified operators. These professionals know the rivers intimately—the hidden currents, the safest lines, the weather shifts that signal danger. Guides also provide crucial pre-trip safety briefings and teach you rescue techniques. I was stunned the first time I learned about "throw bags" — rescue ropes that can save a swimmer in trouble. It gave me immense peace of mind.

Don't let ego push you to go solo or with inexperienced friends. South America's rivers have claimed many ill-prepared adventurers. Good guides not only protect you but also enrich the trip by sharing insider knowledge about local culture, wildlife, and history.

Pro tip: When choosing a tour, ask about their safety record, guide certification, group sizes, and what emergency protocols are in place. It's better to pay a bit more for a reputable operator than to risk your life on a cheap, unregulated trip.

Seasonal River Conditions: Timing is Everything

If there is one piece of third-party advice that truly transformed my river experiences in South America, it's this: Know the river's rhythm. The seasons turn these waterways from tranquil veins into raging torrents, or calm them into reflective mirrors, and each state offers unique challenges and rewards.

The Rainy Season: Wild and Untamed Rapids

The rainy season breathes life and fury into mountain rivers, swelling their volumes and intensifying rapids. I vividly recall paddling the Apurímac during November, when the Andes released their melting snows and rainstorms. The river was a wild stallion—unpredictable, powerful, and exhilarating.

But the rainy season is a double-edged sword. While it heightens excitement for advanced rafters, it can also close access to certain sections due to dangerous floods and landslides. Safety becomes paramount. Always check local river conditions before booking. Many guides will only operate during safer windows or adjust routes accordingly.

In Amazon tributaries, the rainy season means flooded forests and expanded waterways—an entirely different paddling experience. You can float through areas normally inaccessible on foot, encountering birds and mammals drawn to the new aquatic habitats.

The Dry Season: Calm Waters and Wildlife Bonanza

Conversely, the dry season brings lower water levels, making rapids less intense and rivers more navigable for beginners or those seeking a peaceful journey. When I paddled through the Pantanal in dry months, I experienced a different magic—the chance to spot giant otters, capybaras, and caimans clustered around shrinking waterholes, a wildlife spectacle impossible during high waters.

Dry season trips are also better for extended canoe expeditions where wildlife photography and birdwatching are the focus. Water clarity improves, making underwater visibility excellent for spotting fish and aquatic plants.

Insider Wisdom and Practical Advice for Your River Adventure

After many years and countless miles on these rivers, I'm often asked: How do I prepare to get the most out of this adventure without risking safety or missing the hidden gems? Here's what I tell friends, and what I wish someone had told me before my first trip:

- **Physical Preparation Matters:** Even the calmest river trips demand stamina and flexibility. Do some cardiovascular and strength training before your trip, especially if you're aiming for multi-day mountain river expeditions.
- **Pack Smart, Pack Light:** Waterproof dry bags for your essentials, layered clothing that can wick moisture and dry quickly, sun protection, insect repellent, and a water-resistant camera or GoPro.
- **Respect the River's Power:** Never underestimate currents or obstacles. Always follow your guide's instructions, never paddle alone, and learn basic rescue techniques.
- **Embrace Local Culture:** Many river communities are deeply connected to these waterways. Take time to engage respectfully, learn about indigenous traditions, and support local economies.
- **Plan Your Timing:** Consult local experts on the best months to visit specific rivers depending on your preferred activity—wild rapids or calm wildlife exploration.

CLIMBING AND MOUNTAINEERING

I remember the first time I stood beneath the towering Andean peaks, the sheer vertical cliffs rising above me like ancient sentinels guarding secrets millennia old. The air was thin, sharp, and filled with a heady mix of exhilaration and dread. I was there before, caught between the thrill of conquest and the humbling realization of nature's raw power. If you've ever dreamed of scaling some of the most breathtaking volcanic summits and rugged mountains South America offers, this is your definitive guide. With insider knowledge, personal experience, and hard-earned advice, I will take you through everything you need to know about climbing and mountaineering across the Andes—where every step is a battle, and every summit a triumph.

Andean Peaks and Volcanic Summits: Giants of the Southern Hemisphere

South America's spine, the Andes mountain range, stretches more than 7,000 kilometers, home to some of the highest, most dramatic peaks outside Asia. From the colossal Aconcagua in Argentina, the tallest mountain outside of the Himalayas, to the smoking volcanic summits of Ecuador and Chile, this landscape is a climber's paradise and a challenge like no other.

Aconcagua: The King of the Andes

I was there before, standing at the base of Aconcagua, the mountain that commands respect not just because of its height but because of its fierce weather and unpredictable terrain. At nearly 7,000 meters, it is a non-technical but physically demanding climb, often described as a "walk-up" but never underestimate the altitude. The thin air makes every breath a victory and every step a small conquest.

What many third-party questions reveal is a common misconception: Aconcagua is not just a strenuous hike; altitude sickness is the real enemy. Before attempting it, climbers must be thoroughly acclimatized. I spent days training at high altitude camps, constantly monitoring my pulse and oxygen levels. My excitement grew as I moved upwards, but so did the risk of high altitude pulmonary edema or cerebral edema, which can turn fatal if ignored.

The route itself, the Normal Route, offers breathtaking panoramas, but experienced climbers often seek the more technical Polish Traverse or the treacherous Polish Glacier route for a serious challenge.

Volcanic Summits: Cotopaxi, Villarrica, and More

There's a mysticism to climbing active volcanoes. I have scaled Ecuador's Cotopaxi, and the experience was surreal—walking on volcanic scree, breathing in sulfur-tinged air, and gazing down into a crater still steaming from earth's molten heart. These climbs require technical skills, including glacier travel, crevasse navigation, and often ice axe and crampon proficiency.

Villarrica in Chile is known for its exhilarating lava lake views and often requires ropes and anchors to navigate steep volcanic rock. When I joined a guided expedition there, the guide's insider knowledge about volcanic activity was critical; we had to adjust our schedule based on seismic readings.

Volcanic climbing is not for the faint-hearted. The terrain changes quickly, and weather can turn the climb into a treacherous ordeal. But the reward—standing atop a fiery giant with panoramic views of the Andes—is unmatched.

Technical Skill Requirements and Permits: Know Before You Go

Climbing in South America demands more than ambition; it requires preparation, skill, and knowledge of regulations that vary wildly between countries and parks.

Technical Skills: What You Absolutely Need

I cannot stress enough how vital it is to acquire proper technical training before setting foot on high Andean climbs or volcanic ascents. While some peaks like Aconcagua's Normal Route don't require advanced climbing skills, most others do. Glacier travel, crevasse rescue, ice climbing, and high-altitude navigation are essential skills you must master.

My personal experience taught me that no amount of physical fitness can replace technical knowledge. I vividly recall a near-miss on a glacier when I failed to secure my harness correctly. The guide's quick intervention saved the day, reinforcing that technical competence is a life-or-death matter.

For volcanic summits, ice axe arrest, crampon walking, and rope management are non-negotiable skills. If you don't have formal training, I strongly advise enrolling in a certified mountaineering course before your trip.

Permits and Regulations: What to Expect

Every country has its own permit system and regulations for climbing peaks within national parks or protected areas. For instance, climbing Aconcagua requires a permit issued by Argentina's National Park Service, and the fees vary depending on the season and route. Failure to obtain permits can lead to hefty fines or even expulsion from the park.

In Ecuador, climbing Cotopaxi and other volcanoes requires registering with the park authorities and often hiring certified guides. Chile's Villarrica Volcano is similarly regulated, with a strong emphasis on safety and environmental protection.

My insider knowledge from local guides and park officials revealed that these permits are not mere bureaucratic obstacles—they are designed to protect fragile mountain ecosystems and ensure climber safety. Always apply well in advance, and keep copies of your permits handy throughout your climb.

Guided Expeditions and Training Tips: The Key to Success

Climbing alone in these environments is not only risky but often prohibited. Joining guided expeditions is the safest and most enriching way to experience Andean summits and volcanic adventures.

Why Guided Expeditions Matter

I've been part of both independent climbs and guided expeditions. Without exception, the guided trips offered a better chance of success and safety. Guides bring invaluable insiders' knowledge—about route conditions, weather patterns, local hazards, and even the best times to climb to avoid crowds or dangerous storms.

Good guides are also trainers and morale boosters. I remember the last leg of my Aconcagua ascent, when fatigue and altitude hit hard. Our guide's encouragement and expert pacing kept the team together and focused.

When choosing a guided expedition, look for operators with certified mountain guides who have extensive experience in the Andes and hold relevant international mountaineering credentials. Ask for details about group size, acclimatization schedules, rescue plans, and emergency communication capabilities.

Training Tips: Preparing Your Body and Mind

The Andes demand physical and mental resilience. Here's my advice from firsthand experience:

- **Acclimatize Early:** Spend several days at high altitude before your climb to avoid altitude sickness. Consider shorter hikes on nearby peaks.
- **Endurance and Strength:** Build cardiovascular fitness through running, cycling, or swimming. Strengthen your legs, core, and upper body with targeted workouts.
- **Technical Practice:** If possible, train on glaciers, ice, and rocky terrain before your trip. Join mountaineering schools or workshops.
- **Mental Preparation:** High-altitude climbing is as much psychological as physical. Develop coping strategies for stress, fatigue, and isolation.
- **Gear Familiarity:** Practice using all your equipment in controlled conditions so nothing surprises you on the mountain.
- Birdwatching and Ecotourism
- I have to tell you, there is something utterly magical about standing in the heart of a South American rainforest or cloud forest, binoculars glued to your eyes, completely absorbed in the vivid spectacle of avian life. My excitement in those moments is off the charts—the thrill of spotting a rare species, the hush as a flock passes overhead, the intricate songs that fill the air like nature's own symphony. If you've ever asked third-party questions about how to truly experience birdwatching and ecotourism in South America, I'm here with insider knowledge that goes far beyond the basics. I've been there, in the dense jungles, on community-led trails, witnessing birds that few get to see up close, and I want to share everything that made those trips unforgettable, safe, and impactful.

BIRDWATCHING AND ECOTOURISM

Specialty Bird Tours and Community-Led Trips: Getting Beyond the Tourist Trail

- South America is nothing short of a birdwatcher's nirvana. I'm talking thousands of species, from the flamboyant macaws to the elusive Andean cock-of-the-rock. But it's not just about ticking species off your list; it's about the immersive experience. Specialty bird tours are where it's at.

- When I joined a community-led birding tour in the Amazon, it completely changed my perspective. These tours, often run by indigenous or local groups, offer an insider's view that you simply cannot replicate on a commercial expedition. The guides have intimate knowledge of the local habitats and bird behaviors—knowledge passed down through generations. They know the secret roosting spots, migration timings, and even subtle cues of bird activity.

- Many of these tours prioritize conservation. They operate on a model that benefits local communities financially and incentivizes habitat protection. I was fortunate to participate in such a tour in Manu Biosphere Reserve in Peru. The guides were not only passionate birders but also fierce advocates for preserving their environment. Being part of these tours means you contribute directly to conservation efforts, ensuring these birds continue to thrive.

- If you want to maximize your chances of spotting specialty species, such as the Harpy Eagle or the Spatuletail Hummingbird, choosing a community-led trip with seasoned guides is non-negotiable. Their knowledge feels like insider information, elevating your birdwatching from good to legendary.

Conservation-Focused Travel: The Heart of Responsible Ecotourism

- I cannot emphasize enough how critical it is to approach birdwatching with conservation at the forefront. You see, the sheer popularity of birdwatching has its pitfalls. Unregulated tourism can disrupt breeding grounds, scare shy species, and degrade fragile ecosystems.
- My personal experience taught me that ethical travel means more than just following rules—it's about genuine respect and contribution. On one trip to Ecuador's cloud forests, I witnessed firsthand the positive impact of travelers who engaged in conservation-focused travel. We participated in reforestation projects, helped with bird banding programs, and supported local conservation NGOs. These efforts, small as they might seem, create ripples that protect biodiversity for future generations.
- When booking tours or lodging, ask pointed questions. Does the company have partnerships with conservation organizations? Do they educate visitors about local environmental issues? Are there limits on group sizes and noise levels to minimize disturbance? Insiders' knowledge tells me that the best operators have transparent policies and actively contribute to habitat preservation.

Equipment and Timing: Gear Up for Success

- If you want to experience birdwatching the right way, you need the right tools. I remember on my first birding expedition in the Pantanal, struggling with inferior binoculars and missing out on clear sightings. The lesson was clear: quality matters.
- Invest in binoculars with at least eight times magnification and good light transmission. My absolute go-to is a lightweight, waterproof pair with a wide field of view. They allow you to scan dense foliage quickly and catch fleeting glimpses of rare birds.
- A spotting scope can be a game-changer for stationary observation points. During my time in the Galápagos Islands, the scope helped me identify distant seabirds and marine species with incredible clarity.
- Timing your birdwatching trips is crucial. Early morning is prime time when birds are most active, singing and feeding. Many species become less active as the day warms, so plan your excursions accordingly. Seasonal timing is just as important—migratory patterns, breeding seasons, and even fruiting cycles affect bird presence. I had the rare privilege to witness the spectacular macaw breeding season in the Peruvian Amazon, a truly unforgettable spectacle that required precise timing coordinated with local experts.

- Don't forget to bring a field guide tailored to the region. A compact, well-illustrated guidebook or an app loaded with bird calls and photos will immensely enhance your experience.

CHAPTER 11

SUSTAINABLE TOURISM AND CONSERVATION IN SOUTH AMERICAN PARKS

ENVIRONMENTAL THREATS AND PRESERVATION EFFORTS

When I first set foot in the breathtaking national parks of South America, I was overwhelmed not only by the sheer beauty but also by the palpable tension hanging beneath the canopy—the fragile balance between preservation and destruction. Over the years, as I traveled deeper and witnessed both the marvels and the scars left behind, my excitement was often tempered by a profound sense of responsibility. Let me take you behind the scenes with insider knowledge and personal experience to reveal the enormous environmental challenges facing these parks, as well as the heroic preservation efforts spearheaded by local communities and scientists. If you are planning your own visit or want to truly understand the stakes involved, this chapter is essential.

Deforestation, Climate Change, and Tourism Impacts: The Triple Threat

The first truth I learned, often echoed by local rangers and environmentalists during my numerous visits, is that South America's natural parks are under siege. The relentless march of deforestation is a primary driver of ecosystem loss. In places like the Amazon Basin, vast swaths of rainforest are cleared each year for agriculture, cattle ranching, and illegal logging. I was in the heart of the Amazon when I saw how entire landscapes were transformed almost overnight, the vibrant greenery replaced by barren, degraded soils.

But the problem isn't isolated to the Amazon. Coastal wetlands, cloud forests, and even high Andean ecosystems are vulnerable to deforestation and habitat fragmentation. This leads to a cascade of ecological consequences—from loss of species to disruption of critical ecological processes.

Climate change is an ever-growing shadow looming over these regions. During my trip to Patagonia's glaciers, I saw undeniable evidence of glacial retreat that locals described as unprecedented. Seasonal weather patterns are shifting, leading to prolonged droughts in some areas and intense flooding in others. This unpredictability affects wildlife migration, breeding cycles, and vegetation growth. It also threatens indigenous communities whose livelihoods depend on stable environmental conditions.

Tourism, while a powerful economic driver and tool for conservation awareness, brings its own set of challenges. When I hiked through popular parks like Iguazu and Torres del Paine, the sheer volume of visitors at peak times was staggering. Trampling of fragile vegetation, littering, and noise pollution degrade habitats. Unscrupulous operators sometimes prioritize profit over sustainability, causing unintentional but significant damage.

I have had heart-to-heart conversations with park managers who expressed both pride in what they protect and frustration over the pressures they face daily. The triple threat of deforestation, climate change, and tourism impacts is a complex web that requires nuanced solutions.

Protected Area Management and Community Involvement: Guardians of the Land

One of the most encouraging realities I encountered is the deep commitment to preservation through robust protected area management and the empowerment of local communities. Third-party questions often revolve around how these vast parks are managed effectively, especially given their remoteness and scale. The answer lies in an evolving partnership model between governments, NGOs, indigenous peoples, and local residents.

Protected areas like Manu Biosphere Reserve, Pantanal, and Galápagos Islands are governed by detailed management plans that balance access with conservation priorities. I've been privileged to participate in ranger-led programs where I saw firsthand the meticulous work involved—from trail maintenance and visitor education to wildlife monitoring and anti-poaching patrols.

149

The role of community involvement cannot be overstated. Indigenous groups possess invaluable traditional ecological knowledge that informs sustainable land use and species protection. For instance, in the Peruvian Amazon, I joined community stewards who patrol their ancestral lands, blending modern technology like GPS tracking with ancestral wisdom about forest health. These partnerships create a powerful synergy, enhancing both biodiversity conservation and cultural preservation.

In many cases, local communities are the frontline defenders against illegal logging, mining, and wildlife trafficking. Ecotourism initiatives that channel economic benefits back to these communities foster a sense of ownership and incentive to protect their natural heritage. When I stayed at eco-lodges operated by local families, I witnessed how conservation and livelihoods can go hand in hand.

Research and Monitoring Programs: The Science Behind Preservation

To combat environmental threats effectively, robust research and monitoring programs are indispensable. I have always been fascinated by how scientific inquiry translates into real-world conservation action. Many of South America's national parks collaborate with universities, international NGOs, and government agencies to conduct long-term ecological studies.

At Torres del Paine, I joined a field research team studying the impact of pumas on the local ecosystem. The data collected helped refine park policies on predator management and visitor interaction. In the Amazon, camera traps and acoustic sensors monitor elusive species such as jaguars and harpy eagles, providing insights into population trends and habitat use. This kind of insiders' knowledge is priceless for adaptive management strategies.

Climate monitoring is another critical focus. Glacial melt rates, river flow patterns, and temperature variations are tracked continuously to anticipate changes and inform local adaptation plans. For example, in Patagonia, this information has prompted shifts in visitor management during vulnerable periods to reduce human stress on ecosystems.

Visitor impact monitoring is equally vital. Parks use trail counters, surveys, and satellite imagery to assess how tourism affects landscapes and wildlife. These data guide infrastructure development, such as building boardwalks to protect sensitive vegetation or zoning areas with restricted access.

The scientific community is increasingly involving citizen scientists—visitors like you and me—in data collection. Participating in bird counts, plant inventories, or even simple observations can contribute to ongoing monitoring efforts.

During one trip, I found my casual notes on butterfly sightings included in a regional database, a small but meaningful way to contribute to conservation.

RESPONSIBLE TRAVEL GUIDELINES

I still remember the first time I truly grasped the immense power a traveler holds when visiting South America's pristine national parks. It was an eye-opening moment, standing on a trail overlooking the jagged peaks of the Andes, watching a group of tourists unknowingly disturb the fragile ground beneath rare orchids. I was there before, caught up in my own excitement, oblivious to the impact my presence could have. Since then, my understanding has deepened profoundly. Responsible travel is not just a phrase thrown around lightly—it is the very lifeblood of preserving these extraordinary landscapes and cultures. If you've ever asked third-party questions about how to travel ethically and sustainably in these environments, here's my insiders' knowledge, born of experience and refined by years of conscious exploration.

Leave No Trace Principles and Waste Management: The Core of Ethical Wilderness Travel

The Leave No Trace principles are a foundational set of guidelines that every visitor to South America's parks must internalize. When I first encountered these principles on a guided trek through Monteverde's cloud forest, it was like a revelation. These seven principles—plan ahead and prepare, travel and camp on durable surfaces, dispose of waste properly, leave what you find, minimize campfire impact, respect wildlife, and be considerate of other visitors—aren't just theoretical concepts.

They are practical, proven tactics to ensure the wilderness remains untouched for others to enjoy.

One of the most glaring issues I've seen, unfortunately, is waste mismanagement. Plastic bottles and snack wrappers left carelessly can harm animals and degrade the landscape for decades. Even biodegradable waste, if left behind in large quantities, disrupts nutrient cycles and attracts wildlife, leading to dangerous habituation.

In every park I visited—from the Galápagos to Patagonia—I made it a point to carry reusable water bottles and pack out all my trash. It's a simple habit, but the impact is massive. The best operators supply refill stations and encourage visitors to reduce single-use plastics. I highly recommend travelers invest in compact, lightweight trash bags and use them religiously. It is the small personal choices that aggregate into large-scale preservation.

When camping in backcountry or refuge systems, I have seen firsthand how human waste must be managed meticulously. Many parks provide designated facilities or require packing out waste in specialized containers. Follow these instructions precisely, no matter how inconvenient, because failing to do so jeopardizes the entire ecosystem.

Supporting Indigenous Communities and Local Economies: Respecting People and Place

Another critical aspect of responsible travel, which I became increasingly passionate about after multiple trips involving indigenous partnerships, is the conscious support of local communities. South America is home to hundreds of indigenous groups whose cultures, languages, and traditional ecological knowledge are inextricably linked to the landscapes we visit.

Tourism, when managed ethically, can be a powerful tool to sustain these communities. I was fortunate to spend time with the Shipibo-Conibo people along the Amazon River, learning how community-based tourism provided a steady income and incentivized forest conservation. Purchasing handicrafts directly from artisans, staying at family-run eco-lodges, and hiring local guides are not only enriching experiences but also direct ways to support livelihoods.

When you book tours or accommodations, ask detailed questions about ownership and profit distribution. Third-party questions like "Does this lodge employ local staff?" or "Are tours organized by indigenous groups?" can make a huge difference. Genuine community-led projects prioritize cultural preservation alongside environmental protection, and your patronage ensures their sustainability.

It is crucial to approach cultural interactions with humility and respect. Avoid exploitative behaviors such as taking photos without permission or treating indigenous culture as mere spectacle. Engage meaningfully by listening, learning, and supporting initiatives led by the communities themselves.

Volunteering and Citizen Science Projects: Active Participation in Conservation

One of the most transformative experiences I've had in South America's parks was volunteering on a jaguar monitoring project in the Pantanal. Immersing myself in the day-to-day work of conservationists, setting camera traps, and collecting data gave me an insider's perspective that changed the way I travel forever.

Volunteering and participating in citizen science projects are incredible ways to give back during your trip. Many parks and NGOs welcome responsible travelers who want to contribute meaningfully, whether by helping with reforestation, wildlife surveys, environmental education, or habitat restoration.

If you are considering volunteering, be sure to research thoroughly. Look for programs with clear goals, ethical practices, and positive impacts on local ecosystems and communities. Avoid any organization that exploits volunteers for cheap labor or whose activities harm wildlife.

Citizen science projects, often coordinated through apps or local research centers, allow casual visitors to contribute data by recording bird sightings, plant species, or water quality measurements. During a stay in Manu Biosphere Reserve, I regularly logged observations that fed into ongoing biodiversity monitoring. This gave me a sense of connection and purpose beyond just sightseeing.

By engaging in these projects, you not only deepen your understanding of the ecosystems but also support long-term conservation efforts. It's a win-win that enriches your travel and benefits the planet.

FUTURE CONSERVATION INITIATIVES

Having roamed through the lush rainforests of the Amazon, trekked the jagged peaks of the Andes, and paddled along the remote waterways of the Pantanal, I can say without hesitation that the future of South America's national parks hinges on the power of innovation, education, and proactive traveler involvement. When I was there before, witnessing the awe-inspiring beauty and the growing challenges, my excitement was always coupled with a deep curiosity about what comes next. What are the new frontiers in conservation? How can technology and community spirit combine to protect these lands? And most importantly, how can travelers like you become part of this unfolding story? Let me take you inside the cutting edge of preservation efforts with insights from insiders and my personal experience on the ground.

Innovations in Park Management: The New Wave of Conservation Technology and Strategy

The landscapes of South America are vast and complex, making traditional management methods often insufficient. From the steamy jungles of Manu to the sprawling fjords of Patagonia, park authorities have started embracing a new wave of technological innovation that is nothing short of revolutionary. When I first heard about the use of drones to monitor illegal logging in remote sections of the Amazon, I was instantly captivated. Being able to cover hundreds of square kilometers in hours instead of days is a game-changer. I witnessed drone pilots in action during a trip to Brazil's Pantanal, where these flying sentinels help spot poachers and track wildlife movements in real-time.

Beyond drones, artificial intelligence and satellite imagery are being harnessed to detect deforestation and habitat changes with unprecedented accuracy. These tools empower rangers with real-time data, allowing swift interventions that would have been impossible just a decade ago. I was fortunate enough to join a workshop with park managers in Ecuador, where they demonstrated how machine learning algorithms analyze images to identify threats and even predict patterns of illegal activity.

On the ground, innovations in eco-friendly infrastructure are taking hold as well. Trail design now incorporates erosion-control materials and natural drainage systems to reduce visitor impact, something I witnessed firsthand at Torres del Paine. Solar-powered ranger stations, bio-toilets, and waste recycling initiatives are becoming standard, ensuring that even remote outposts minimize their ecological footprint.

Community-based monitoring apps allow local residents and indigenous groups to report sightings or suspicious activities instantly. During a field visit to Manu Biosphere Reserve, I participated in training sessions where locals learned to use smartphones for conservation purposes—a fusion of ancient knowledge and modern technology that truly inspired me.

Education and Outreach Programs: Cultivating a Conservation Ethic for the Future

In my years of travel and volunteering, I have come to realize that no conservation effort can succeed without widespread education and outreach. After all, the long-term protection of these parks depends on cultivating a conservation ethic among visitors, local communities, and future generations.

Several parks have launched innovative education programs that go beyond simple awareness. For example, in Iguazu National Park, interactive visitor centers use immersive technology to simulate the park's ecology and threats, engaging even the youngest travelers in understanding their role in preservation. I attended one such session, and the excitement among children was palpable—evidence that education rooted in experience can truly inspire.

Local schools in communities surrounding parks are integrating environmental studies into their curricula, often with support from NGOs. I met teachers in the Andes who brought students into the field for hands-on learning about native plants, water conservation, and wildlife behavior. This approach fosters pride and stewardship from a young age.

Outreach programs also target tourism operators, encouraging them to adopt sustainable practices and educate their clients. During a conference in Peru, I observed how guides shared best practices for responsible tourism, which travelers then carried into the field. This ripple effect multiplies conservation impact far beyond the parks' borders.

Social media campaigns and storytelling play a vital role too. Personal stories from local custodians, scientists, and travelers—like the ones I share—help humanize the

155

conservation mission. When people connect emotionally, they are more likely to act responsibly and support preservation financially or through advocacy.

How Travelers Can Contribute to Preservation: Your Role as a Catalyst for Change

Here's where things get personal. I have always believed that travelers are not just observers but active participants in the ecosystems they visit. The question I hear most often from third parties is: how exactly can I, as an individual, contribute meaningfully to conservation while traveling?

First and foremost, your choices in how you travel matter. Opt for tour operators and accommodations that are certified sustainable, support local communities, and follow strict environmental protocols. Ask detailed questions about their conservation efforts and be vigilant about avoiding any activity that harms wildlife or habitats.

Engage in citizen science programs whenever possible. Even simple acts like recording bird sightings, participating in reforestation projects, or helping with wildlife monitoring can add up. I still cherish the memory of planting trees with an indigenous group in the Amazon—a small act that felt like a giant step toward healing the forest.

Consider volunteering your time or skills during your trip or even after you return home through remote projects. Many organizations welcome support in research, fundraising, or education. Being part of a community dedicated to preservation expands your impact beyond the trip itself.

Financial contributions to trusted conservation initiatives are another powerful way to help. When I was involved in supporting a jaguar corridor project in the Pantanal, I witnessed how targeted funding could create protected migration routes essential for species survival.

Most importantly, become an ambassador for conservation. Share your experiences, educate others about the challenges and solutions, and advocate for policies that protect these treasured environments. Your voice, amplified by personal stories and authentic passion, can inspire others to act.

CHAPTER 12

COMBINING NATIONAL PARKS WITH CULTURAL AND SCENIC HIGHLIGHTS

NEARBY CULTURAL SITES AND INDIGENOUS COMMUNITIES: WHERE NATURE AND HUMANITY DANCE TOGETHER

When I first set foot near one of South America's iconic national parks—let's say the breath-snatching landscapes of Machu Picchu just outside Manu Biosphere Reserve—I was struck immediately by a powerful realization: the parks don't exist in isolation. They are surrounded, cradled, and deeply intertwined with the lives, histories, and spirits of indigenous peoples and ancient civilizations. This connection was not some distant theory for me—it was something I *lived*, *breathed*, and *felt* coursing through every step I took.

You see, third-party questions often come my way: "How do I experience the wilderness without feeling like I'm just an outsider looking in? How do I respect the people who have lived here for centuries while still being an explorer?" I get these questions because I've been there, too, wondering how to approach it all without overstepping. Here is where insiders' knowledge matters most, and I want to share everything I've learned—both through personal experience and through countless conversations with indigenous leaders, local guides, and cultural ambassadors.

Ancient Ruins: Echoes of Civilizations Past

The ruins scattered around South American national parks are not just stones piled high; they are silent storytellers of empires that once thrived in harmony with these landscapes. Think of the sacred citadel of Machu Picchu overlooking the Urubamba River valley. When I first stood on those terraces, my heart raced with the sheer magnitude of human ingenuity intertwined with nature. The precision of Incan stonework seemed otherworldly, perfectly suited to withstand earthquakes and erosion over centuries.

But it's not only the Incas. Near the Pantanal, the ancient Jesuit missions tell stories of cultural collision and blending. The petroglyphs near Ischigualasto National Park in Argentina transport you to a time when indigenous peoples carved their worldview into stone. My guide, a local archaeologist, shared stories that made me see these ruins not as abandoned relics but as living memories.

If you want to delve deep, I cannot overstate the importance of hiring a local guide— someone who can bring these ruins alive with legends and historical context. It's like having a key to a secret room. Without this, you risk walking past these treasures without really *feeling* them. I was there before, wandering solo, and the difference between a guide-led tour and a casual stroll is night and day.

Villages and Traditional Festivals: Immersing Yourself Respectfully

The villages nestled on the outskirts of parks such as Torres del Paine or Manu are vibrant ecosystems of culture and tradition. On one unforgettable trip, I stayed with a Quechua family near the base of Ausangate Mountain in Peru. Their warmth and the way they weave their history into daily life fascinated me. Their weaving patterns told stories of mountains, rivers, and ancestors. The local festivals, often synchronized with agricultural cycles, are not tourist spectacles but deeply meaningful rituals.

For anyone eager to experience these cultural highlights, a word of advice: approach with humility and curiosity, not entitlement. Third-party travelers often ask me how to avoid being the annoying "cultural tourist." My answer is simple: listen more than you speak. Participate respectfully, ask questions with genuine interest, and always seek permission before photographing or joining rituals.

During the Inti Raymi Festival in Cusco, I was lucky to witness ancient sun worship ceremonies that predate the Spanish conquest. The excitement and reverence were palpable. It was an insider moment I will never forget, and it reminded me that cultural experiences rooted in respect enrich your journey far beyond sightseeing.

Engaging Respectfully with Local Cultures: A Guide from My Own Experience

Respect is the cornerstone when blending nature excursions with cultural encounters. You might wonder how to engage authentically without causing offense or seeming superficial. My personal experience in the Amazon taught me that the simplest acts—learning a few words in the native language, dressing modestly according to local customs, or sharing a meal—can build bridges instantly.

I remember vividly a conversation with an elder in a Shipibo community, where I asked about their views on conservation. She spoke with passion about their ancestral responsibility to protect the forest and how tourism, if done right, can support their efforts. This kind of dialogue is invaluable for any traveler. Third-party questions such as "How do I ensure my visit helps rather than harms?" often reveal a lack of understanding about local priorities. I learned that supporting local artisans by purchasing their crafts directly and hiring community guides are powerful ways to contribute.

Be mindful of cultural protocols—many communities have sacred sites or ceremonies that are not open to outsiders. Pushing boundaries here can cause deep hurt and harm relationships that took generations to build. My excitement about cultural immersion was always tempered by the awareness that I was a guest in someone else's home.

Cultural Tours and Experiences: Curated Journeys into Heritage

If you are someone who thrives on storytelling and history, booking a cultural tour with local experts can transform your trip. I have joined several such tours, from the weaving cooperatives in the Andes to cacao harvest experiences in Venezuela, and each time I left with not just souvenirs but knowledge and friendships.

Tour operators increasingly partner with indigenous communities to offer authentic experiences that also generate sustainable income. For instance, in Ecuador, some tours combine guided hikes in Podocarpus National Park with visits to Kichwa villages, where you can learn traditional farming techniques or participate in music and dance.

When selecting a cultural tour, seek operators who demonstrate transparency about their community partnerships and emphasize sustainability. Avoid packages that treat cultures as "exotic entertainment." I personally vet tour providers by reading reviews, asking pointed questions, and sometimes even contacting communities directly if possible.

My advice to you: blend cultural tours with your national park adventures. Spend a day trekking in cloud forests, then take the evening in a village learning about local cosmology and crafts. This layering of experience transforms your journey into a holistic exploration of place.

Bringing It All Together: Practical Tips for Combining Parks and Culture

I know from my own journeys—and from the numerous travelers I have guided or advised—that balancing natural wonders with cultural immersion requires careful planning and an open heart. Here are some precise, actionable recommendations from my experience:

- **Research Ahead**: Identify key cultural sites near the parks you plan to visit. Look for festivals or market days that can enrich your visit. Knowing what to expect reduces surprises and increases respect.
- **Hire Local Guides**: There is no substitute for insiders' knowledge. Local guides open doors to hidden stories, explain cultural nuances, and act as bridges between worlds.
- **Time Your Visit**: Festivals and traditional events often follow seasonal or lunar calendars. Plan your trip to coincide with these moments for a truly immersive experience.
- **Practice Ethical Photography**: Always ask permission before taking photos, especially of people or sacred rituals. Be ready to accept a "no" gracefully.
- **Support Local Economies**: Purchase handicrafts directly, eat at community-run restaurants, and choose accommodations that employ locals.
- **Learn Basic Language Phrases**: Even a simple "thank you" or "good morning" in Quechua, Guarani, or Mapudungun shows respect and opens hearts.
- **Be Patient and Observant**: Cultural immersion takes time. Slow down, listen, and absorb.

SCENIC ROUTES AND ROAD TRIPS

Pan-American Highway Segments and Scenic Byways: The Spine of a Continent

The Pan-American Highway is more than just a road. It is the pulse line of South America, stitching together diverse landscapes, cultures, and ecosystems over thousands of kilometers. When I first embarked on a segment of this sprawling route—driving from northern Colombia through Ecuador and down to Peru—I was overwhelmed by the sheer variety of what I encountered.

Picture this: one moment, you're winding through misty Andean highlands, with snow-capped peaks towering overhead. The next, you descend into lush cloud forests where colorful hummingbirds flit between flowers, and nearby villages invite you to taste fresh cheese and sip local coffee. Driving here isn't about speed; it's about savoring every curve, every vista.

Insiders' knowledge tells me that the best way to approach the Pan-American segments near national parks is with an itinerary that allows for spontaneous stops. Trust me on this one. Some of the most remarkable discoveries came from turning down an unmarked side road—perhaps a tiny gravel track signposted only by a hand-carved wooden sign—and stumbling upon a hidden waterfall or a centuries-old chapel nestled among eucalyptus trees.

Hidden Gems and Off-the-Beaten-Path Destinations: Beyond the Tourist Trail

Third-party questions often ask: "How do I avoid the crowds and truly experience authentic South America?" My answer is simple: get off the beaten path. While iconic sites like Iguazu Falls and Torres del Paine are must-sees, the real magic often lies in lesser-known places.

I recall a journey through Patagonia where I veered away from the main highway and into a remote valley dotted with abandoned sheep stations and wildflower meadows. There, the silence was so profound that even the wind seemed to pause. I camped under a dazzling night sky filled with stars you won't see in the city.

Or take the lesser-known coastal route along the Pacific in Chile, south of Valparaiso, where quaint fishing villages and secluded coves provide perfect stops. Here, you can savor fresh seafood and chat with local fishermen about their daily lives. No tourist buses, just genuine encounters.

If you want to explore these hidden gems, I recommend getting a reliable local map and talking to residents. They often reveal secret spots only known to those who have lived in the region for generations. Plus, many of these hidden locations have small, family-run hostels or eco-lodges where you can rest and recharge before hitting the road again.

Trip Planning and Logistics: Making the Journey Smooth and Enjoyable

From my experience, successful road trips in South America hinge on meticulous planning and smart preparation—but also on flexibility. You need a robust plan but also a spirit ready for adventure.

Vehicle Choice: I can't stress enough the importance of selecting the right vehicle. Some stretches are paved highways, but others quickly turn to gravel or dirt roads. I personally opted for a sturdy 4x4 rental when traveling through the Andes and Patagonia, which gave me the freedom to explore remote areas without worrying about getting stuck.

Permits and Documentation: Depending on your route, border crossings can be a challenge, especially if you plan to cross between countries. I was once held up for hours at the Chile-Argentina border, but having all my documents, vehicle permits, and insurance in perfect order made the wait less stressful. Check local regulations in advance, and make sure your insurance covers multiple countries.

Fuel and Supplies: In remote regions, gas stations can be few and far between. When I drove through the Amazonian foothills, I always filled up the tank at the last major town and kept extra fuel in a jerry can. Pack plenty of water, snacks, and a basic first aid kit. Some stretches have little cell coverage, so having offline maps and a GPS device is crucial.

Accommodation Booking: While spontaneity is great, during high season it's wise to book at least your first few nights in advance, especially near popular parks. I combined camping with stays in cozy lodges, balancing ruggedness with comfort. Apps and local travel forums helped me find reliable options.

Safety: South America is generally safe for road travelers, but common sense prevails. Avoid driving at night on unfamiliar roads, lock your doors, and keep valuables out of sight. Connecting with local tourism offices or police can provide updated info on road conditions or advisories.

Insider Advice: How I Was There Before and What I Learned

Reflecting on my road trip along the Chilean Patagonia's Carretera Austral, the journey was nothing short of epic. Driving through endless forests, past fjords shimmering under the afternoon sun, I felt like I was exploring a hidden continent. Each day brought new surprises—glaciers calving into turquoise lakes, wild horses galloping across vast plains, and nights warmed by campfires beneath auroras dancing faintly overhead.

The thrill of the road was matched only by the joy of meeting locals—gauchos who welcomed me to their estancia for an evening of stories and fresh empanadas. These moments, far from guidebooks or tourist trails, became the highlight of my trip.

If you're planning a similar adventure, my top tip is to embrace the unexpected. Be ready to slow down, ask locals for advice, and dive into small towns where the real culture thrives. Keep your itinerary flexible—some of my best experiences happened when plans changed at the last minute.

MULTI-PARK ITINERARIES AND EXTENDED ADVENTURES

Combining Rainforest, Mountain, and Coastal Parks: The Ultimate Multi-Park Experience

I remember planning my first multi-park expedition across South America, grappling with third-party questions about how to maximize time without feeling rushed. Here's the truth: It's all about balance and smart sequencing.

Imagine starting your adventure in the **Amazon rainforest**, where the lush canopy teems with life, then ascending to the majestic Andes for crisp mountain air and sweeping vistas, and finally unwinding along a pristine coastline with vibrant marine biodiversity. This trio of ecosystems delivers a rollercoaster of sensory delights, from the steamy humidity and cacophony of tropical birds to the icy winds and rugged terrain of highlands, finishing with the salty breeze and crashing waves of the ocean.

For example, a classic route might begin in Peru's Manu Biosphere Reserve or Ecuador's Yasuni National Park to experience the rainforest's extraordinary biodiversity. After immersing yourself in the jungle, you could fly or drive to Cusco and then trek or drive through the Andes to visit Machu Picchu and surrounding mountain parks like Huascarán in Peru or Cotopaxi in Ecuador. Wrapping up, you might head to the coast—Galápagos Islands in Ecuador or the rugged Chilean coastline—to snorkel with sea lions or explore volcanic islands.

My insider tip: Allow at least ten days for a multi-park itinerary like this. It might sound like a long time, but believe me, you'll want the breathing room to soak in each ecosystem's unique magic. Rushing through the parks risks missing their essence entirely.

Adventure Sports and Cultural Immersion: Fueling the Thrill and Heart of Your Journey

Here's where the excitement really cranks up. South America is a playground for adventure seekers and culture lovers alike. From personal experience, blending adrenaline sports with authentic cultural immersion transforms a trip from good to unforgettable.

In the Amazon, I went kayaking down calm tributaries under the moonlight, guided by indigenous community members who shared their ancestral knowledge about the forest's healing plants and spiritual significance. That night, the jungle came alive with sounds that words can't capture, and the stars above seemed closer than ever.

In the Andes, my adrenaline soared during a multi-day mountaineering expedition on volcanic summits, pushing physical limits while absorbing breathtaking panoramic views. Between climbs, I stayed with Quechua families in remote mountain villages, joining their traditional festivities and savoring home-cooked meals. This combination of physical challenge and cultural connection anchored the trip in a way no checklist could replicate.

On the coast, I kayaked around Galápagos islands, spotting blue-footed boobies and snorkeling alongside graceful sea turtles. Local guides emphasized sustainable tourism practices, explaining how their community works tirelessly to protect this fragile marine ecosystem.

Advice for your trip: Seek out tour operators and guides who prioritize sustainability and community engagement. This not only enriches your experience but also ensures that your adventure contributes positively to local livelihoods and conservation efforts.

Family-Friendly and Group Travel Planning: Crafting Inclusive and Memorable Journeys

Traveling with family or a group adds another layer of complexity and joy. I've been there, organizing trips that cater to diverse interests and energy levels while keeping logistics smooth.

When planning multi-park trips with kids or mixed-age groups, consider parks with varied activity levels. For instance, start in a rainforest lodge with accessible trails and wildlife watching suitable for children. Then move to mountain parks with moderate hikes and cultural experiences like visiting indigenous communities or traditional markets. Finally, end with coastal or beach destinations where relaxation and water activities cater to everyone.

Some parks, like Torres del Paine in Chile or Iguazu Falls in Argentina and Brazil, offer ranger-led programs and family-friendly facilities, including safe walkways and educational centers. These parks blend awe-inspiring scenery with structured activities that engage younger travelers without overwhelming them.

For groups, especially those interested in adventure sports, tailor your itinerary to include options like zip-lining, horseback riding, or gentle rafting, ensuring everyone's comfort and safety. Booking accommodations that offer group rooms or family suites makes a huge difference in convenience and bonding.

My personal insight: Communication and flexibility are keys to success. Before you set out, discuss everyone's expectations and physical capabilities openly. Also, build in rest days and allow for spontaneous detours—some of the best memories arise from unplanned discoveries.

Practical Tips for Making Multi-Park Itineraries Work Flawlessly

Now, let's get into the nitty-gritty. Here's how I ensure my multi-park adventures are not only thrilling but seamless:

- **Plan with Geography in Mind:** Choose parks that are logistically feasible to connect. For example, pairing Machu Picchu with the Amazon basin in Peru is doable via Cusco. Trying to link the Pantanal in Brazil with the Galápagos in Ecuador in a short trip, on the other hand, requires more flight time and careful scheduling.
- **Book Internal Flights Early:** Air travel is often the fastest way between distant parks. I always book flights weeks ahead to secure the best prices and connections, especially in peak seasons.
- **Pack Versatile Gear:** Weather and terrain vary wildly. Layered clothing, waterproofs, sturdy hiking boots, and lightweight swimwear can handle rainforest humidity, mountain chills, and coastal sunshine. Don't forget insect repellent and sunscreen.
- **Stay Hydrated and Eat Well:** Altitude sickness is common in highlands, so acclimate slowly and keep hydrated. Enjoy local cuisines—Andean potatoes, Amazonian fruits, coastal seafood—because food is part of the adventure.
- **Insurance and Health Precautions:** Given the diverse environments and activities, comprehensive travel insurance covering medical evacuation is essential. Vaccinations like yellow fever for Amazon regions, and malaria prophylaxis where advised, are non-negotiable.

CONCLUSION

EMBRACE YOUR SOUTH AMERICAN ADVENTURE IN 2025

There is something profoundly moving about reflecting on the vast and breathtaking diversity of South America's national parks. From the misty cloud forests where the rarest birds sing unseen, to the thunderous cascades of Iguazu Falls, from the remote deserts of Atacama to the watery wilds of the Pantanal, these places are not mere tourist destinations. They are living, breathing sanctuaries—woven into the very fabric of our planet's future. Having been there before, standing at the edge of glaciers or listening to the low growl of a jaguar in the twilight, I can tell you firsthand: these parks are priceless treasures, and their protection is urgent.

REFLECTING ON THE DIVERSITY AND IMPORTANCE OF SOUTH AMERICA'S PARKS

I often get asked by fellow travelers and friends why South America, of all places, stirred my soul so deeply. Third-party questions like "Why go so far?" or "What makes these parks special?" arise naturally. And my answer is simple yet profound. These parks are living textbooks, classrooms of the natural world that showcase evolution, resilience, and the delicate balance that sustains life on Earth.

Conservation here is not a buzzword. It is the very heartbeat of these regions. In every park I've visited, I've seen the tireless work of rangers, local communities, and scientists—many of whom have spent their entire lives protecting these wild places. Without their stewardship, the jaguars would lose their homes, the cloud forests would fade, and the waters that sustain millions would run dry.

My excitement to share this guide is rooted in the hope that you, the reader, become part of this vital movement. Responsible tourism, when done right, is one of the most powerful tools for conservation. By walking softly, respecting wildlife, supporting indigenous communities, and spreading awareness, each visitor becomes a guardian of the land.

If I may be bold, your journey in 2025 is more than just travel. It is an act of stewardship, an investment in the future of these parks and the species within them. The call of the wild here is a call to protect, to cherish, and to inspire others to do the same.

CONTINUING YOUR JOURNEY BEYOND THIS GUIDE

The adventure doesn't end with closing this book or arriving home. It is just the beginning. I remember vividly, after my first extended trip through Patagonia and the Amazon, how I found myself craving more—more knowledge, more connection, more ways to contribute.

To that end, I highly recommend diving into additional resources tailored to your interests. Whether that's books on ecological research, documentaries on South American wildlife, or travel blogs by seasoned explorers who've walked the trails you dream of, these materials will deepen your understanding and fuel your passion.

Connecting with conservation organizations is another way to extend your impact. Groups working on the ground in South America welcome volunteers, citizen scientists, and advocates. From reforestation projects to wildlife monitoring, these efforts need people who are informed, dedicated, and ready to engage meaningfully. When I volunteered in the Pantanal, for instance, I witnessed firsthand the difference individual action can make—and the incredible friendships that blossom in those shared endeavors.

Sharing your stories, whether through social media, travel journals, or casual conversations, is equally powerful. People listen to personal experience more than facts alone. Your excitement, your photos, your tales of wild encounters can inspire others to explore and protect these treasures. Imagine the ripple effect—one journey turning into many, one voice encouraging an entire community.

FINAL THOUGHTS AND TRAVEL INSPIRATION

As I wrap up this guide, I want to leave you with a heartfelt invitation. Whether you are a seasoned adventurer or a first-time traveler stepping into the unknown, South America's national parks offer a sanctuary for your spirit, a challenge for your body, and a classroom for your soul.

Remember these essentials as you embark:

- Respect the land and its people. Every footprint matters, every dollar spent should support sustainability.
- Prepare meticulously but embrace spontaneity. Some of the greatest moments come from unexpected encounters.
- Prioritize safety without losing your sense of wonder. Equip yourself with the right gear, stay informed about health precautions, and listen to local experts.

- Keep an open heart and mind. The diversity here is not just biological but cultural—a mosaic of indigenous wisdom, colonial history, and modern resilience.

I was there before, standing beneath a sky glittering with stars so bright it seemed the universe itself was celebrating. I felt the pulse of the rainforest, the chill of the mountain breeze, and the spray of the ocean's waves. Each moment etched a lifelong memory.

This is your moment now. Go boldly, explore widely, tread lightly, and return richer in spirit and understanding.

South America awaits—and the adventure of a lifetime is yours to claim.

Printed in Dunstable, United Kingdom

66395325R00100